alvin's laws of life

5 steps to successfully overcome anything

by Alvin Law

Library and Archives Canada Cataloguing in Publication
Law, Alvin, 1960-
    Alvin's Laws of Life: 5 Steps to Successfully Overcome
        Anything / Alvin Law.

ISBN 0-9739450-0-1

    1. Self-Actualization (Psychology). I. Title.

BF637.S4L359 2005   158.1   C2005-906468-4

Publisher
AJL Communications Ltd.
273 Sunmills Drive SE
Calgary, Alberta T2X 3E6 Canada
adlaw@telusplanet.net
www.alvinlaw.com

Project Management and Editing
Debbie Elicksen, Freelance Communications, Calgary, Alberta

Design and Layout
Nadien Cole Advertising, Calgary, Alberta

Cover and Section Photographs
Mitch B. Hippsley, Yorkton, Saskatchewan

Printing
Friesens, Altona, Manitoba

Alvin's Laws of Life – 1st Edition

Printed and Bound in Canada
Copyright 2006
Second Printing 2007

table of contents

dedication

For Mom and Dad: what I know is because of you.

For Vance: because being a dad taught me what my parents couldn't.

For Darlene: for your love, acceptance, and encouragement. It has been worth my while.

I remember the first time I ever had a speaker touch my heart, back in Yorkton, Saskatchewan, my hometown. Yorkton was a great community to grow up in, but when I was a teenager, I didn't appreciate it. It was small – small enough that we didn't get big concerts or shows.

In the fall of 1976, the students of Yorkton Regional High School were told we were going to have a world-class motivational speaker come to our school. I remember the event like it was yesterday. Coming to school that morning, I was curious about what we were going to see. We certainly were not on the regular motivational speaker circuit, and I didn't know anyone else that had ever sat in front of a motivational speaker. It was not so different than any events or assemblies we had had in the past. Whenever we had an assembly, we would file down to our theatre and act like respectful teenagers. Our principal, Mr. Matthews, was very dedicated to motivation and positive thinking and was always looking for new ways to inspire us to be better. We weren't really surprised to be having something so different being presented to us.

We learned that assemblies, although not always very interesting or entertaining, were almost always better than being in class. Mr. Matthews introduced our guest. This well-dressed gentleman walked out onto the stage and started to talk. By the time I was sixteen, I was more than a little cynical of lecturing. But this man truly was amazing. He was powerful, passionate, and the most polished presenter I had ever seen in my entire life. I sat in the audience in awe of him, not knowing what to think. This was the happiest human being I had ever seen in my entire life; I hated him. He was so happy he was annoying. Do you know anybody like this? I bet he was happy twenty-four hours a day and drove everyone around him crazy.

As if that wasn't bad enough, he got about a half hour into his program and then changed his pace. He became real intense, real focused, and real quiet then said, "Do you teenagers realize that these are the best days of your life!" Okay, I don't know what your teenage life was like, but the first thought that hit my head, 'Oh-oh, that's not good news!' I was sixteen years old. I had no arms. I was living in rural Saskatchewan where nothing ever happened. I had greasy, poofy, ugly hair. I had acne everywhere. I had buckteeth with braces, and my name was Alvin! Man, if these are the best days of my life, maybe I should quit right now!

I always tell that story for a couple of reasons. For one thing, it's true, and as a funny story, it's great for breaking the ice. More than that, I think it's about credibility. Adults are always telling teenagers to enjoy that time in their life, to relax and not take things so seriously. There is plenty of time in the future to worry about getting a university degree, to have a serious relationship, buying a house, and the list goes on. What we forget is that we are giving this advice out of hindsight. I don't know anyone who sailed through their teenage years on a magic carpet with no anxieties about life, school, and relationships. It is in our teenage life that we learn about these things and how to deal with them.

I keep that story in mind when I talk to any audience – not just teenagers. I try to relate my experiences so that others can learn from them, but more than that, I want people to listen to my stories and think about similar stories in their own lives. Because we all have a similar story – it's called life.

So, what I did was develop what I call "Alvin's Laws of Life." Get it? Alvin Law, Alvin's Laws? Five steps to help me successfully get through life. Do I wish I had these "Laws" when I was growing up? You bet! Actually, when I look back, I did have these laws; I just didn't know it yet. It was because of what I went through in life and learned along the way that I can now look back and realize it was what I went through that made me the person I am. Now it's up to me to be the person I want to be.

Attitude is more than just being positive – it's a way of looking at life, ours and everybody's. It is said to be everything because it *is* everything. It defines who we are and what we become.

Learning is the greatest gift we give ourselves. It can transform us from nobody to somebody and is the great equalizer. To not learn as much as we can is to disrespect the gift of life. In learning, we must also ask questions. That's good because people need to listen more and talk less. There is knowledge all around us; we just have to listen for the answer. To listen is to learn, and to learn is to grow.

Value your life and spirit. Too many people live another "V," that of victim. It's true, bad things happen to good people, and there are victims. The trouble is there's no answer to the question, "Why me?" Even worse, victims often get stuck in their past when what they need is to live for today and move toward the future. When you focus on moving forward, you never know what you'll discover. Everyone has value – finding it, that's the trick.

imagination is the key that unlocks the power of potential. It is not owned by the young, but they are best at using it. It defines the difference between obstacles and possibilities. Imagination leads to dreams, and dreams make life worth living. Dreams can come true...this I know.

Never give up! Easy to say, hard to do. The biggest enemy we will ever have we encounter every time we look in a mirror. Yet mirrors do not reflect who we truly are – our lives do.

chapter one

imagine

You're about to read a great story. In fact, make sure you make a point of remembering who you are right now, because I promise when you are done, you'll be different. Will you be perfect? No such thing. If you think you're already perfect, good for you. I can relate because I feel really close to perfect, which is a major problem. Seriously, I started writing this book when I was thirty-five years, old and now I'm forty-five. Do the math. I am a perfectionist, and it's not my fault. (Notice how I slip into lack of accountability, a perfectionist's trait?) By the way, I hope you have an open mind because this isn't just another self-help book. Don't get me wrong. I think it's great that people buy such books because they (you, perhaps) feel a need to get out of a rut, fix a pattern of bad decisions, or just try to improve.

The trouble is, there is no magic pill. My parents used to say, 'Life is what happens to you and what you do back!' They didn't make it up, but they believed the words. I tell every group I speak to that I am completely aware of the near lunacy of the expression, 'It's better to have a positive attitude than a negative one.' Duh! That's so obvious. The problem is, and it's a good problem, certain forms of attitude can make a huge difference in overcoming all those negatives that get hurled at innocent bystanders all the time. I may not have the answers, and I plan on doing more than simply make observations. But trust me, this is great story, and the best part is, it's real.

I get noticed. When you have no arms and you use your feet for everything, you tend to attract attention. Actually, I get a kick out of it most of the time, especially because our *politically correct* society says it's impolite to stare. To throw a little light on it for a second, picture me in a rib joint (this happens in most restaurants, but ribs are particularly disgusting) ingesting a full rack of those babies slathered with that thick, gooey, and incredibly tasty sauce, like at Corky's in Memphis. I hold each rib between my big and depending on its size, my second, third or even all the toes on my right foot (I'm right-footed). I rest my heel on the table edge or my left knee (hip waders would be good here) and gnaw on the bone until it's clean. Then my favorite part,

lick and suck each toe until they're clean. Hey! You okay? Look, I'm not going to pull any punches in this book because that's not who I am. What's funny is, if you met me, or better yet, became an acquaintance, you'd find I'm pretty humble. I just hate all this pussyfooting around. If I saw someone pigging out on ribs (pardon the pun) with their feet, I'd look too. I'd probably wave and smile, but I'd look. You don't see someone like me every day. That is the point.

Living life means facing it, every day. Some days, we see something we haven't seen before. In fact, that's an intriguing way to look at this whole book. Seeing something for the first time can be a profound human experience – good and bad. When it's good, it can be the most heart-warming feeling there is.

For example, I saw pictures of the Sydney Opera House in Australia many times, but seeing it in person the first time was amazing.

My wife and I love to hike. Sometimes, we'll walk for miles without seeing anything but bush or field and then…poof! The most tremendous view appears, and you get shivers up your spine. The world *can* be so beautiful.

I saw "Ground Zero" in New York, not long after the World Trade Center was destroyed by gutless terrorists who killed thousands of innocent people in the name of religious motivation. I felt a shiver there too, and it wasn't good. I didn't know anyone who died there, but I felt immense sadness. I've been sad…a lot, but that was a new kind of sad, something I had never felt.

Humans are emotional beings, so our minds are profoundly affected by our heart and soul. Those three things are going to be stretched as you read this. I hope it's in a positive way, because as you know, life isn't always positive. It's easy to have a positive attitude when everything is hunky-dory (great word, huh?). It's not so easy when that big pitcher in the sky throws a serious curveball at you.

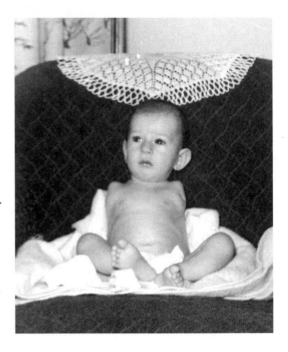

Imagine you're my mom. One day your life is pretty typical. You've got two sons. Your husband has a solid job. You've just moved to a new town and have your first new home. The next day, your whole world changes as you welcome a new member of the family. His reality shatters your somewhat idealistic life. This baby has no arms. Although you've seen a lot of things in your life, you've never seen anything like this. Picture her reaction. Now, imagine what you would do. Obviously, this is a bit of a setup and just knowing that I can eat ribs with a particular zest for life is a clue. The point is, this really happened.

I guess I should come clean here. My mom didn't give birth to me. Hilda and Jack Law were foster parents. I landed on their doorstep because I was given up at a week old for reasons that for so many years seemed obvious. The Laws were foster parents who knew nothing of my history due to privacy rules. They would provide a home for me until a suitable adoption would come along. Thirty years later, I would meet the woman who gave me my life.

Their new home was a two-bedroom bungalow of just under a thousand square feet. I guess they thought they had a little extra space, so they opened their home to unwanted and abused children. They added a self-contained suite in the basement and took in more. They were moderately religious and believed that living with strong morals and values meant living it, not just talking it like so many existing in hypocrisy. Life had been good to them. They wanted to give back, especially Hilda. She loved children. Together they had raised two boys: John and Terry. In 1960 (the year I was born), they had been married for thirty years. Hilda was fifty-five, Jack was fifty-three. Instead of planning their retirement, buying a condo in Florida, and purchasing white shoes, they took in a pathetic, sick, extremely handicapped baby boy who they called Alvin. That would be me.

Imagine how my mother felt the first time we met, the first time she held me, the first time she considered my reality. Imagine it. If you were to ask her about it, I guarantee she would say I was the ugliest baby she had ever seen. Then she would laugh out loud. The laugh would always end with a tear or two, wiped away with the ever-present tissue stuck in the cuff of her sweater. She was incredibly humble and unselfish. How she really might have felt she kept to herself.

This first section is about *Attitude*. If there were ever a great example of it, it's my parents, especially my mom. They had the best all-round attitude of anyone I have ever met in my life. I can guarantee they never read a self-help book, attended a seminar, or watched an infomercial on TV. You don't just *learn* attitude; you use it. Much of what I know about attitude I got from Mom and Dad Law. Even though people say I'm amazing, I think they were amazing. I know that now. I didn't know it then. But I also don't think Jack and Hilda Law knew it either.

is for attitude

*Attitude is more than just being positive
– it's a way of looking at life,
ours and everybody's. It is said to be
everything because it is everything.
It defines who we are
and what we become.*

chapter two
history 101

I love the fact that in talking about *Attitude,* I can use my parents as an example. But before I get too far, I want to discuss a rather profound part of my story. As mentioned, I get noticed, and over the years, the reaction I get has changed. Where I used to be viewed with a degree of disgust, most people are inspired by my abilities. Every now and then, it becomes quite personal.

I was on a flight somewhere. If I can, I prefer an aisle seat on the right side of the plane. I have to travel for my work. I try to be philosophical about it but some days, I just don't feel like traveling. I suppose it's common for frequent flyers, but where most people can simply blend in with the rest of the passengers, I don't exactly blend. If I had a dollar for every time I've had to tell people what happened to me, I'd be Bill Gates' neighbor. I try to be accommodating. This particular example was different. It was a 6:30 AM flight, and all I wanted was to read my book and be left alone.

As fate would have it, there was an empty middle seat. An older woman sat by the window. I'd managed to avoid any conversation for over an hour, had a couple of cups of coffee to wake me up, and just as I thought I'd get away clean, the lady, who'd been watching me the whole time (on and off) made eye-contact and simply asked, "Thalidomide?" For me, it's always intriguing when someone remembers that word. It usually evokes a conversation, which again, I try to patiently conduct, but something told me this was going to be different. I told her it was, and she continued.

"I don't want to bother you, but I just had to know because I've been sitting here having a serious time of reflection."

She went on to tell me that she got pregnant in 1961. It was her first baby, and she was quite young and very intimidated. Her stress, she believed, contributed to her morning sickness. She wasn't doing well. Her doctor suggested a specialist who gave her a sample of this brand new *wonder drug* from Europe. She didn't realize what it was at the time because thalidomide was relatively new to Canada. She took these pills home, put them on the counter in her kitchen, and as she described to me, "Stared at them for days." Something told her not to take them, even though the doctor assured her they were safe. She then choked back her tears, and with the most sincere expression, reached over and touched my knee and said, "Thank God, I never took a single pill because I was blessed with a healthy, normal baby."

Can you imagine all the ways I could take that? Yet, in her mind, she had a good reason to be thankful. I couldn't blame her. In truth, I wouldn't wish having a deformity on my worst enemy. After her declaration, we talked for the next two hours. I told her about my considerable knowledge of the drug and its history. I told her about my life, my parents, my wife, and family (she did cry then). Not surprising, we talked a lot about attitude.

I think *attitude* is a choice we make of how we see things. The over thirteen thousand-recorded thalidomide victims were real. There is no way to put a positive spin on that. I won't go into detail about the legacy of the drug that was banned worldwide in 1963. If you want to know more, I'd suggest a book called *Dark Remedy* by Trent Stephens and Rock Brynner. It is indeed, a dark account of a terrible era in human history. Thalidomide, according to the book, may have killed as many as two hundred and fifty thousand babies. Nothing positive there, although I've actually had people tell me, at least they didn't live. Yikes!

I'll discuss the victim concept in a later section, but one thing I want to bring up is for most of my life, I was unaware it was thalidomide that kept my arms from growing. All I knew was I didn't have them. In 1987, I was invited to join a task force organized by Canada's War Amps organization to investigate what had happened to well over a hundred Canadian thalidomide children. It was a fascinating experience.

The task force studied dozens of files documenting lives that were decidedly pathetic. These lives were not just those of the deformed babies, but also their families. A majority saw alcohol, drugs, and other forms of abuse. Several mothers had even committed suicide. It was disturbing. It made me think about my mother, the one who gave me away. Even though I had to know about me, I also had to know about her. My wife pushed me somewhat because it was difficult to make the call, but I did it in 1993. I met Sophie.

Meeting my birth family, which is my choice of term because I think it takes much more than simply giving birth to earn the title of Mom or Dad, wasn't like on TV. I found it awkward, very awkward. My wife and I arranged the meeting with Sophie and several of her family members in her home in Melville, Saskatchewan. They were strangers to me, but I was not a stranger to them. They knew of me because I'm somewhat famous in the province. If you know anything about Saskatchewan, that's pretty easy. They had lots of questions, and I encouraged them to tell me about their lives. After all, an important motive was to attempt clearing up the past so we could *all* move forward. After some reluctance, Sophie and her family started to talk. We listened. It was a very sad story.

Sophie and Peter Paholko were farmers. They were practically impoverished. Their farm had no power, running water, or creature comforts of any kind. They had two small children when I showed up. They also had Peter's mother living with them. She actually owned the land. When I was born, that only began the tragedy. Doctors predicted my complete dependence on people for life…that's right, life. They provided no hope for any future quality of life and suggested the best plan was for my institutionalization, where I could receive proper care. As compelling as those reasons, the most startling one came from Grandma.

Being a Ukrainian Orthodox Catholic (fact, not criticism), she viewed my deformities as a message from the devil and bringing me home would curse the family, the land, and perhaps most important, her. So she refused to let me be brought home and literally forced them to give me up. Sophie told us it was a decision she had regretted every day of her life since, and if you would have been there, you would know she was telling the truth.

This was definitely one of the weirdest days of my life. I guess it's like that for everyone who finds his or her birthroots. You can't help but imagine what your life may have been and the impact of what it wasn't. My birth father died in the early 1980s, in part, because of how much my being given up weighed on his mind. My siblings, Alan and Elaine, remembered many good times during their youth, but also experienced the change my birth, then departure, had on the home. They told me how they even blamed me for ruining their lives, as they knew it. Their parents, especially their mother, were irreparably damaged by that drug. There was nothing, absolutely nothing, they could do. At the same time, there was an immense respect for what I had accomplished. In a weird twist, there was also an eerie recognition that my life's challenges were because of something their mother did. Complicated, to say the least.

When we met, we lived only ninety minutes away by car in Regina, Saskatchewan. Now, we live much further away, so we don't connect as often as we should. Recognizing that, we invited Sophie to come for a visit by herself and stay a few days. On the second day, we were alone together for the first time ever. She got quite emotional, began crying, and told me she should have been stronger and took me home. It was such a powerful moment because I knew she was sincere. I decided to be the same.

I told her she needed to stop thinking that. First of all, nobody could turn back time, and regret is a very harmful emotion. Second, and perhaps most important, she was witnessing the *final product,* so to speak. She did not see what it took to bring about my new reality. As uncomfortable as this was to say, being a farmer, wife, and mother of two other children, she was not in a position to commit so much of her life to mine.

As fate would have it, Hilda Law was.

chapter three

curiosity is good for all cats

I'm a dad. Don't try to figure out how that happened. Just go with it, okay? Seriously. It seems I evoke much curiosity in everything I do. I remember one of the first speeches I gave. I was a disc jockey in Regina, Saskatchewan, and one day, I was invited to a career fair at a local junior high school. I wore my black vinyl jacket with *FM92* emblazoned on the back. In my best radio voice, I talked to a bunch of thirteen year olds about the radio business. After fifteen minutes, I asked if there were any questions. A kid in the front row raised his hand and asked, "How do you go to the bathroom?"

Good question, really, although not one you may have ever got, huh? I guess I've pretty much heard them all. Over the years, I've had different answers to some questions, of course, because I've not only gained perspective, I've learned things - many at an age much older than most people – that simply involve daily routines. I didn't learn to dress myself completely until I was twenty-eight years old. Imagine that obstacle in your life. Yet, with all my moments of feeling helpless, none surpassed the feeling I had the first time I held my son (I'm sure I'm not alone on that one). He was five minutes old. The doctor put him in my lap while he worked on his mother. I just stared at him. For people that doubt whether miracles happen, watch a baby being born. Yeah, I know. There's a scientific and biological explanation. Please, get a life! Babies are miracles, period.

Even though I'd heard the story many times, as mentioned earlier, Mom said the first thing she thought when she saw me was how ugly I was, I was sure there was more. One time after my child was born, I brought it up again, but said I'd heard the *ugly* joke enough. What *did* they feel?

I remember their reaction more than their exact words. They laughed. I wasn't sure if it was laughing at their memory or my question.

What Mom said was simple. They had no plan for keeping me. It really was a job in a sense. They would look after me until a permanent home was found. Who knew? Yet, I propose that emotion was significant.

Imagine all the parents of the thalidomiders who brought home *their* new baby. It doesn't even have to be that same scenario. Our society paints a picture of the perfect baby. Anything less is, well, less. We're getting better as a society in embracing all new life, but park yourself in 1960 for a moment.

There are some religions that still believe a birth defect is a curse from the gods and those inflicted should be hidden from society. In 1960, institutionalizing such people was common and not just because of religion. That stigma was the dominating factor in all the thalidomiders' lives. I have heard true stories of many thalidomide babies who were never taken out of their homes, for years. Some of them literally lived in a basement or back rooms and their existence was denied. Horrific? Of course, but a true mark of the era.

Consider this. The Laws were not rehabilitation experts. They weren't even formally educated past their early teens. They were, however, veterans of life. If I were to guess, because I truly don't know, they were different than most parents. They were grandparents. They saw life differently. They were older. They were wiser. They were likely able to see me differently than even my own birth parents.

My foster parents' attitude was at first, work-like. They were caregivers, especially Hilda. Her job was to simply make sure I was fed, changed, and generally tended to. I was definitely given lots of attention. The overriding emotion was sympathy. No surprise. Even at middle age, I don't expect people to see me and say, "No arms? Excellent!" I actually expect sympathy. When someone doesn't act that way, it does throw me off, but is a nice change. My so-called disability is *very* unusual. As I have grown older, I have become so accepting of the notion that ninety-nine percent of the population has never met someone without arms. Just the whole notion of *no arms* is so difficult to imagine. When people react to me, I'm okay with that, but I had to learn to be okay with that. So did Mom.

Mom's tendency, at first, was to, pardon the pun, baby me. In part, because of the predictions of the doctors, she carried me everywhere, held me all the time, and rarely left me alone. I suppose I seemed even more vulnerable. As a foster parent, her responsibility was to protect me. But Hilda Law hadn't had an infant around everyday since the 1930s. She and Jack already raised their family and settled into a bit of a routine. True, they were operating a foster home for a while, but they were very active people. My dependency was no problem at first, but then it stretched into months. I was becoming a very clingy baby. There may have still been sympathy, but something else was happening.

Remember, this was supposed to be temporary. Social workers were actively pursuing a permanent adoption. One day, I was taken to a potential home. That lasted three days. Apparently, I was miserable. I cried most of the time and my difference was just too different for these young parents. So, they brought me back. I guess I calmed right down. I was *home*. A couple of weeks later, another potential home popped up. Again, I was taken away from the Laws. This time, it lasted only two days. When I was brought back, I was a mess. Yet again, I seemed to calm right down. But something else seemed to have occurred. It appeared we crossed the line from foster parents and temporary client to *family*.

Completely out of character, Jack Law took the social worker aside and said, "We can't keep going through this. If you come and get him again, don't bring him back!" Wow!

As it turned out, another potential home never materialized. It appeared I wasn't going anywhere, ever again. Although the paperwork wasn't filled out yet, whether fate or just circumstance, Jack and Hilda Law had their third son, and I had a family. I believe that day was my true birth. I also believe that the attitude in that house changed that day. Instead of passing the time and simply providing my care, now things were different. It was time to chart my future. If there was one thing about Jack and Hilda I would one day discover, failure was not an option. Yet, to succeed, one must first fail. Perhaps the most vital distinction was so complicated, but at the same time, so simple. This baby was born for a reason. But what could that be? The adventure was about to begin.

chapter four

what's your box?

One of my vivid memories of our home in Yorkton was the root cellar. It was a tiny room under the stairs that was cold and dark. On its shelves were hundreds of jars full of the best-preserved food you ever tasted. Mom canned a lot. She canned everything. Thus one of my parent's joys was the garden. We had a huge garden, and although it was pretty, it wasn't a *designer* garden. It was like the Laws, a working-class garden.

Food from a Mason jar has no equal. I do know canning is a lot of work and requires focus and timing. Hard to pull off when you have an armless dependent baby on your hands.

I suppose Hilda must have decided that if they had this pathetic kid, perhaps the best formula was to get back to a sense of *normal*. It was time to can tomatoes, but what was she supposed to do with me? She had an idea. There was an empty cardboard box sitting on the floor in the kitchen that used to hold the Mason jars. She took my baby blanket, placed it in the box, and sat me inside. I just sat there. In fact, I even smiled. I guess I liked the box. Mom wasn't stupid. She started putting me in the box all the time. Putting me in the box may have substituted as a mini-vacation. She was always right there where I could see her, as I guess that was all I needed to know – that she was there. It was, I suppose, practical, but it soon would end up being more than that.

A few days later, I was back in my box. For reasons that only Mom could explain, she tried something. She took me out of the box and put me on the floor. I just sat there. I didn't fall over. I just sat and smiled at her. I mention this a lot, but when Mom told the story, she often got tears in her eyes. The box didn't disappear, but day after day, she would take me out of the box, and I just sat there, every time, just happy. Remember, I wasn't supposed to be able to sit up, ever.

It was a couple of weeks later. I had one of my routine appointments at the doctor's office. Mom took me into the examination room, put me on that little bed, and I just sat there with a big toothless grin. The doctor came in, the same one who said I would never do anything, including sit up and said, "He's sitting up! What did you do?" Mom replied, "I put him in a box!"

Naturally, Mom took great pride in proving the doctors wrong. This isn't a giant *raspberry* at the medical community, but the truth is important. They never gave Mom any hope. I don't know why they did that, but Mom lived with hope, or better put, *faith.* She also had another reason to trust her instincts.

When I first came to stay with the Laws, I was very weak. I couldn't keep anything down. I don't know if that was from thalidomide, but I threw up everything I consumed. I was even sent to a Saskatoon hospital that specialized in infant care. Although they stabilized me with intravenous, they never solved the problem. I came back, and soon after, took a backwards step to where I was before. My brother, Terry, had similar problems, and Mom had come up with a *formula.* It was from the farm. Fresh cow's milk and *Bee Hive* brand corn syrup. It worked. As soon as I drank it, I didn't throw up. Before you knew it, I was gaining weight. Is this a story or what? Even I am amazed at the obvious. Hilda Law was a special woman, but she was the last person to ever admit it. I think Mom invented humility. But I believe there is a wonderful point to be made.

I'm actually a bit famous, just a bit. My story has been documented many times, the first time, when I was a little over one year of age. The press heard via the provincial grapevine, or more appropriately, wheat vine that there was a newborn in Yorkton without arms, whose foster parents taught him to use his feet for hands. It was a good story. So they interviewed my mom.

The reporter asked her to describe what it felt like to take care of a baby without arms. She replied, "That's a dumb question. How do you think it feels? It's weird. Wouldn't it be weird? How do we usually pick up a baby? By the arms. He gets dropped a lot!"

The reporter apparently didn't laugh but instead just asked another question. "How did you teach him to use his feet?"

"He did!"

"Pardon me?"

"He taught me!" said Mom.

"Excuse me, how can a baby teach you anything?"

"Obviously, you're not a parent. Babies teach us tons of things!"

"I still don't get it."

Mom explained that one day she walked in my room, and I was dangling my favorite teddy bear by its ear between my first two toes on my right foot and smiling the biggest smile she had ever seen. She then said, "It's like he was saying, 'Look Mom. This is the secret!' You see sir, we were doing what so many people did – both to him and to themselves – we looked at the wrong thing. We were looking at what he didn't have instead of what he did. Once we changed that, everything changed!"

Confidence is an elusive yet obvious emotion. Having confidence in the face of so much opposition is not easy to come by, but perhaps it's a clue. If one has faced similar obstacles in the past, it provides a reason to believe one can overcome them yet again. I believe Mom used that to guide her to the next step, and it would be a biggy.

Instead of focusing on all of the things I would never do in my life, she started imagining the possibilities.

For reasons only Mom could explain, one day she decided I needed to test my boundaries. I am sure this was not a definitive plan but one of possibility. What if I could have my own baby bottle? Her theory was simple. What if she put me in my crib at bottle time, put my bottle on a big feather pillow, and laid me on my side? Why couldn't I drink? It was a great idea, except I kept rolling over. I was very good at rolling over. You know the game kids play, rolling down hills? I always won that game! Never one to quit, she put pillows behind my back to keep me from rolling. That solved the problem. I could drink on my own. For my mom, that was a very big deal. But even she could not predict what was going to happen next.

A few days later, after several *bottle times,* I was in my crib having my bottle, but Mom heard giggling. She came into my room, and much to her surprise, I was sitting up in the corner of my crib holding the bottle between my feet, sucking on it, having a great time! Imagine her reaction. Again, I don't believe she expected anything, but there I was. She was even more curious, so she took me out of my crib, sat me on the floor, put a few toys in front of me, and waited to see what I would do. Without thinking about it, I reached out with my toes, grabbed a toy, and started to play with it.

Alvin at 16 months putting coins in a piggy bank.

I can almost picture her that day. A whole year of mixed emotions, frazzled nerves, and what definitely had to have been serious second guessing the decision to take me in. This was truly a victory of Olympic proportions, but there would be no medal presentation, no national anthem, and no press to record the event. Nope. Just a mom, her baby, and for the first time, an imagination of the future.

section II - learning

is for learning

*Learning is the greatest gift we give ourselves.
It can transform us from nobody to somebody
and is the great equalizer. To not learn as much as
we can is to disrespect the gift of life. In learning, we
must also ask questions. That's good because people
need to listen more and talk less. There is knowledge
all around us; we just have to listen for the answer.
To listen is to learn, and to learn is to grow.*

chapter five
have feet will travel

When I originally developed my *Laws,* I had "L" stand for *Love.* My instinct was that my mother's love and love in general was vital. I still think it is. But, I decided that *Learn* should be the "L." Sadly, not everyone has the love I had and have. But everyone, and I mean *everyone,* has the ability and the necessity to learn. I believe it to be the most underutilized and most important of the human dynamic. Remember that expression, 'Give a man a fish, feed him for a day; teach a man to fish, feed him for a lifetime.'

Obviously, I was not the first person on earth born without arms. Although with the reaction I usually get in public, I may as well be. That didn't sound bitter, did it? I'm not bitter, but as I have already mentioned, sometimes it would be nice to go one day in the outside world without *that look.* The reality is, people like me are very rare. While that means the inevitable attention, it also means little or no resource material. This was also the early 1960s, so the folks couldn't just scroll to a search engine on the Internet and look up *no arms.* What *did* they do?

Well, I had learned to use my feet. Step one accomplished!

For step two, my parents decided on a remarkable, yet common sense approach. You've heard of comfort zones, right? Mom may not have used these exact words, but what she and Dad basically did was expand their knowledge zone (okay, for sure Mom wouldn't have used those words), while at the same time, applying the one they currently had. Simply put, if I was going to use my feet instinctively, then why couldn't that instinct be applied to the natural curiosity babies all have, that my brothers had?

So began the journey. What makes it that much more quaint is how everyday stuff would be my teaching tools. Mom continued to use the box as a strength and balance builder, not to mention, it was a great baby-minder so Mom could get some things done. Every phase would be as close to regular baby stuff as possible. Mom was a seamstress and had countless empty thread spools. I would learn to pick them up and eventually put them in my mouth. When that happened, cookies and crackers replaced them in order to teach me to eat with my feet. My parents had very generous friends who knew we were poor, so they would buy us baby stuff. One of the most important gifts was a *Jolly Jumper.* Just in case you don't know what that is, it's a harness attached to heavy gauge springs that are, in turn, attached to a hook that attaches, in our case, to the door frame between the living room and the kitchen. I'm sure they don't make them anymore, probably because they weren't really safe. The Jolly Jumper was said to improve the strength of babies' legs and feet: important for all babies, vital for baby Alvin.

My whole life has been a big deal. Whether in the extreme of the horror of having no arms or the amazement of driving with my foot, I am like a documentary in progress. I appreciate the curiosity. People often ask me if I've been in *Ripley's Believe It Or Not,* a museum and of late, a television show. As of this writing, no. I have had my share of media exposure, including three award-winning TV documentaries and several shorter features. One even won a coveted *Emmy.* I have allowed my life story to be told primarily to educate the public. My wife would probably tell you that two of my favorite things are a microphone and a camera, even better when they are together. I can't lie. The attention is nice, but I still believe my motives are not that different than Mom's.

If you *learn* to do the ordinary, then it is proof that the extraordinary is just another step away.

the learning begins

I don't remember learning to hold my bottle, learning to walk (which I didn't do until I was almost two), or learning to talk, which I have been accused of doing more of than anyone else in the free world. In fact, the first actual *memory* I have is of sewing. No, not with a fancy high-tech, programmable sewing machine – with my toes. Now imagine using a needle and thread with your toes without a thimble.

According to Mom, I was about three years old when I learned to sew. Mom was a seamstress. She actually made extra money making clothes, doing hems or cuffs, etc. She either did it by hand or with her trusty Singer treadle machine. Nothing fancy for her. As you can guess, I spent a lot of time with Mom, and not because I was overprotected. In fact, the opposite was true.

Although she gave some guidance, I pretty much *learned* on my own. But *learning* isn't just figuring it out the first time; it's about failing and failing a lot. It's also about not quitting when you fail. It's about practicing…a lot. Practicing to get past the failure and to get better and better. People are astounded at how easy I make using my feet look, but it isn't easy. Like I said earlier, try it. I often get my audiences, especially youth, to try printing their name with a pen or marker between their big and second toes like I do. It's a funny idea and even funnier for me to watch. But to be serious, the only way to make the impossible possible is to start by trying, and no matter how hard it is, to not stop because it's hard.

I am truthfully and constantly amazed at how strong my parents were in not wavering from their mission. They had some unorthodox ways of teaching me to perfect my skills. Dad was a heavy duty mechanic and used to bring home various sizes and weights of nuts and bolts from work. I would screw them on and off for hours at a time. I had to do chores…yes kids, those dreaded chores. As I got older, I had to make my bed, *every morning,* pick up my toys every night, vacuum the carpet every week, mow the lawn (using my chest), shovel snow (same method), take out the garbage…in my teeth – that was nice. I even remember the first time Mom said, "Time to start doing the dishes!"

"How am I supposed to do that?" I replied.

Her answer, "How am I supposed to know? You're the one without arms. You figure it out!"

That was Mom. She and Dad loved me, but sometimes those who love you make you do things you don't necessarily understand.

Families are not a democracy. I constantly hear parents tell me that young people have lost respect for them…duh! When we allow children to be treated as equals, we begin the slide right there. Of course, it isn't a hundred percent the parents' fault. Pop culture, which in itself isn't all bad, has made a significant contribution.

My point is, many people have, perhaps unknowingly, given up the very respect they feel is now lacking by teaching kids they have a parallel voice in the family unit. More important, kids have *learned* the fine art of manipulation and many have their parents wrapped around their little finger.

There was *no* democracy in the Law household, but I never, ever questioned whether I was loved. However, in a strange twist, one thing I would have loved to have a say in would be my first hint of trouble to come.

chapter seven
if it ain't broke…fix it

I remember coming into the kitchen one morning when I was around three (the same time I learned to sew). Mom was talking on the phone. When she hung up, she gave me her patented great smile. I'll never forget what she said.

"I have great news sweetie…you're going to get arms."

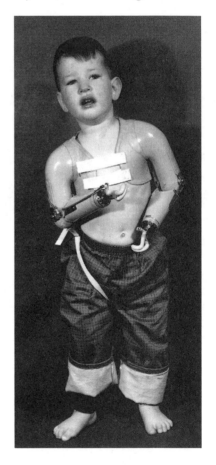

You just remember a day like that! I thought we were going shopping! In reality, I was going to a hospital, but not because I was sick, although one could suggest that I was about to be given a theoretical *cure* for what ailed me.

A few weeks later, Mom and I boarded a Saskatchewan Transportation Corporation bus headed for the capital city of our province: Regina. We checked into the Plains Hotel three hours later. It was my first stay in a hotel. We took a cab, also a first, to the Wascana Rehabilitation Hospital. I had been there before, but I didn't remember because I was so young. I had been to a few clinics where I had been the subject of deformity discussions. This time, there was no clinic, but I was about to experience something I would eventually learn to hate.

We entered the hospital. For some reason, I remember Mom being very positive and encouraging. I would find out later it was an act, but that day, it was like an adventure. We went to an office where I met a couple of doctors and a therapist. Mom signed some documents and then the bombshell came. I was staying there. Mom was not. Imagine that. Maybe you can but most cannot. I will never forget that feeling. In a large part, my age dictated that this was new to me, but it was still a shock. It was typical of Mom. Before I had a chance to freak out, she gave me an explanation.

She told me that an auntie of mine was sick, and she had to go home to look after her, so these people were going to take care of me. Since Dad had yet to completely buy into Mom's new plan, it wasn't a surprise that he wouldn't be looking after me. I can still recall how convincing she was, perhaps even more now because it was such a lie. She even added that while I was there, I would be trying out a new activity that we didn't have at home – one that was only available in the hospital. Like a shot I blurted out, "The arms!" I remembered. Mom just smiled and said I was right.

She reminded me she had to catch the bus home. We needed to take my things to my room and get me settled so I'd be comfortable. I was pretty lucky, actually, because in most rooms, there were four to eight beds. But not in mine…just two. I would have a roommate, but he wasn't there just then. A roommate? I had to share? I was pretty much an only child. My parents two biological sons were born in the 1930s, so sharing was something I did with my neighborhood friends. I don't think I was very good at it. Oh well, maybe he'd be fun.

Mom put most of my clothes in the lower drawers, hung up what didn't fit, and told me it was time for her to go. I tried to be brave but didn't pull it off. I remember the first tears and with all my strength, I couldn't pull them back. That began a small flood. Mom held me in those tender but strong arms and asked me to be tough for her. My circle of influence was somewhat limited, but like most kids my age, I would do anything for my mom, so I cranked up my courage and was able to turn off the taps long enough for her to leave. That was 1964, yet I can still see her walking down that hospital hallway, all dignified and strong, one last wave and she was gone.

Not all *learning* is good. Children, in particular, *learn* some of life's cruel ways much too early and often. I have never blamed the medical or rehabilitation community for what I went through. Others, like Canada's Aboriginals, who were stolen from their families and plopped down in residential schools run by whites where they were stripped of their language, their culture, their history, and perhaps most important, their dignity – they had every right to be bitter, as do I, I suppose.

Perhaps some of the best education we can get is from lessons taught by life. Mitch Albom makes a reference to that in his excellent book, *Tuesdays With Morrie,* (also one of my favorite movies) that we learn as much from what hurts us as what loves us. In an immediate way, I *learned* the routine at the hospital, the use of my new prosthetics, and even a few new games from my roommate, Kelvin. Somewhat ironically, Kelvin was born without legs because of thalidomide, although we never knew the linkage. Kelvin and I would eventually cross paths again later as a result of the thalidomide task force. When we did meet, we spent a lot of time comparing notes of our similar lives. Kelvin's parents (his mom took the drug) were eerily similar to mine in that they refused to mourn the loss of his legs and focused on his strengths. Not all the natural parents were lost in the wake of their tragedy, but I digress.

I also *learned* that Mom did come back. Over the next twelve years, every time she left, she would return. I *learned* to hate hospital food but loved the attention I got from countless nurses, therapists, and even a couple of doctors (although most kept their distance).

Perhaps the best thing I *learned*, above everything else, was how much I hated being handicapped. Soon, I would also *learn* that my choice in that matter would be a long time coming.

chapter eight

school...bring it on

By the age of six, there wasn't much I needed to do that I could not do. I still had the arms, but I only wore them an hour a week. When I did, I hated them. They were heavy and cumbersome. They had these big metal hooks for hands and were controlled by cables than ran from the hooks up each arm and down to a strap on each leg that would, when I bent or straightened my body, pull open or close my *hands*. When I did wear them, Mom would often put a patch over my eye so I could run around the neighborhood playing pirate (shiver me timbers).

By the age of six, I and most of my friends on Fifth Avenue North in Yorkton were ready for school. We pretty much had two choices, Burke Public School, a couple of blocks away, or St. Alphonses Catholic School (where I would be going), right across the street from our house. Was I lucky or what? The fact we were Protestant wasn't something I had considered, but I was six. What did I know?

St. Al's was having an open house for new students and their families. Little did I know that Mom had a plan. She knew, although I didn't, that my birth family was Catholic, and they had asked if it were possible that I be a practicing Catholic. The social workers probably would have fixed that by placing me with a Catholic family, but since there weren't any lineups to take me home...well, beggars can't be choosers.

So off we went to the open house. I want you to picture my folks. In 1966, Mom was sixty-one. Dad was fifty-nine. Mom was five-foot-four, Dad, almost six-four. Mom weighed one hundred sixty-five pounds (she was a solid woman in those days); Dad was around two hundred forty. Mom was a homemaker and foster-mother; Dad was a heavy-duty mechanic. As different as they were, I was so proud of them.

I find it interesting that parents often believe their young kids actually care about the same things they do. Okay, let's try that again. Do six year olds care about where their parents work, how big their house is or the neighborhood it's in, what hood ornament is on the family car, or what designer label is in the collar of their clothes? I think not. Please remember all my observations are highly generalized and intended for reflection. Having said that, our Western culture needs a serious slap in the head because what you own never defines who you are, but so many people believe that. I guess I come by my biases honestly. This story is one of my favorite "real-life" examples intended to remind people what they take for granted.

So we toured the school, met some teachers, had some hot chocolate, coffee, and doughnuts, and predictably, I was getting so excited, I couldn't even find the words. I couldn't wait to start school. I didn't really know what was going on, but it seemed we had to go meet "the boss." Before you knew it, we're in the principal's office with the door closed. Dad was on my left in his overalls from work, Mom on my right in one of her very limited nice dresses. I was in the middle, dressed to impress, complete with blue blazer and bow tie. If it was Mom's plan to address the religious thing, of which I had no knowledge, times two, she didn't get a chance to spring it because the principal said something I will never forget.

"I'm sorry Mr. and Mrs. Law, but he can't come here."

Dad abruptly replied, "We live right across the street!" (Maybe Dad didn't know the plan either.)

The principal explained it wasn't that simple. At which point, Mom started to talk about them being Protestant. But before she got to bring up my birth family, he cut her off and said that *wasn't* the problem. "So what was it?" someone asked (I don't remember who because I was still stuck on *he can't come here*).

"He needs to go across town to the school where kids like *him* go."

"Kids like who?" (Protestant Catholics, perhaps.)

"Crippled kids like him," blurted the somewhat impatient headmaster, while pointing at me.

"He's not crippled," shot back my mom.

"He has no arms, what do you call that?"

"Alvin!"

Good story, huh? Important point time: This is not about the principal or St. Al's for that matter. It *is* about the time. Hard to believe that not that long ago, children with disabilities weren't allowed to go to regular school. By the way, this is not to suggest the special schools were useless, and it most certainly is not to suggest we don't need modern special education. Oddly, it's the word *special* I find fascinating because the connotation is often the opposite of the reality. Time to rant for a bit.

Why is diversity something we even have to discuss as an idea? Now, if someone were to suggest we start diversifying with the animal world, yeah, pause for lots of thought, but people are people!

In case you didn't catch that, I have a slight issue with racism, prejudice, social hierarchy, heck – any kind of discrimination. It has absolutely no place in our modern, twenty-first century, theoretically enlightened world. What is society's fascination with labels?

One of my heroes, Martin Luther King, spoke of dreaming of a country and a people, where one is judged not by the color of their skin but the content of their character. Mind boggling to think he was killed because of such radical ideas.

It was an interesting moment of my life that is frozen in Technicolor to this day. Mom, by now, had clearly become disturbed. She even got tears in her eyes, as this seemed something she hadn't considered. Dad seemed to pick up on this. But first, I think you need to know about Dad.

Dad was born in England and came to Canada in 1923 when he was sixteen years old. Unbelievable. Why? He came alone. The very short version of the story is a buddy and him decided they would come to Canada, where in the 1920s, encouraged immigration. If they came, they would be provided training programs and good wages. Dad was a typical impatient teen who wanted to see the world, and his imagination led him to Canada. Problem was, his buddy pulled out at the last minute. Dad, being stubborn, came alone. He trained as a mechanic, and to help supplement his income, he also became a heavyweight boxer. He was good at it, even won several championships.

In the principal's office, he saw Mom's tears. I remember this like it was yesterday. He looked at Mom, looked at me, and said, "Hilda, I think it's a good time for you to take a break. Take the boy. Get him another doughnut. Get yourself another coffee. The principal and I are going to have a little chat!"

Okay, you need to know something here. Dad was not a new-age modern kind of guy. He was, with respect, a redneck. He was a very hard-working blue collar laborer who worked extremely hard as a mechanic and service manager for a big truck and farm implement dealership in Yorkton, called Mickelson's Truck and Implements, an International Harvester outlet. Mom had been my caregiver and took me to all the clinics, the hospitals, and had been a stay-at-home mom. Dad was a good man, but he was about to enter a new level.

Twenty minutes later, Dad emerged from the principal's office and exclaimed, "Kid, you're going to school tomorrow!"

For years, I thought my dad beat up the principal. Nope! What he did was stand up for one. I never knew what actually transpired until many years later. I asked my father several times over the years, but he seemed uncomfortable to discuss it. That eventually changed, and when he told me the story, I finally knew the truth and why he kept it to himself.

Dad looked at the principal and said, "You know, I didn't want him either. We'd raised our family, and just look at us. We should be slowing down. But his mother's a remarkable woman. She wanted to take in foster children, probably because that house across the street is our first new home. She decided we had some extra space (it was under a thousand square feet). So, because I have such respect for her – we've been married since 1930 – I agreed. Most of the foster kids have been older and abused in various ways. It is truly disgusting what some people do to their own children. Fortunately, my wife is a miracle worker. The kids were able to find permanent adoptions so things were working out okay. But one day, they brought over the saddest looking child I'd ever seen. I took one look and thought, why would we take him? He's going to be nothing but a burden. But sir, he kind of grows on you. You have to give him some time, and if you do, you'll see there is more good than bad. Besides, we do live across the street, and he needs to come here. No matter what you've always done, you need to change it. We did and it was worth it!"

Just as Martin Luther King stood up for equal rights for African Americans (something that today seems logical but then seemed ludicrous), Dad also stood up for a principle. He was my Martin Luther King. The big world changed socially as a result of King's efforts, and my world changed, thanks to my dad. He was my hero.

section III - value

is for value

*Value your life and spirit. Too many people
live another "V," that of victim. It's true, bad things
happen to good people, and there are victims.
The trouble is there's no answer to the question,
"Why me?" Even worse, victims often get stuck
in their past when what they need is to live for
today and move toward the future. When you focus
on moving forward, you never know what you'll
discover. Everyone has value — finding it,
that's the trick.*

chapter nine

reality

Let me say this right here. There are *victims*. Every day in the news, there are stories of people, often completely innocent people, who are the victims of real life. It is horrible, and I won't suggest for a minute that my life can be compared to that of, for example, those who have had a loved one murdered. Especially children. Whenever I tune the television to CNN and witness an unfolding drama of a missing child, my stomach churns. I'm a dad; I can't even imagine.

What I want to address is what happens when you are a victim. Remember, they did call us the thalidomide victims. Trust me. I have met some thalidomiders whose life story is truly heart wrenching. There is *no* answer to the question, "Why me?" Bad things happen to undeserving people all the time. I feel it enters the category of the unexplained mysteries that accompanies humanity. I offer my views as one of the motivations for writing this book in the hopes that I can help people put their own lives in perspective. But that alone hasn't been easy. Believe it or not, I've had a hard time completing this project. The idea that I have the *answers* to life is a bit weird for me, yet when I step outside myself and attempt some objectivity, I must have done something right.

As of this writing, Dr. Phil is a huge celebrity with a very successful television show where he offers his profound knowledge of human psychology. For some, I'm sure he comes off as insensitive. People appear on his show with real life problems, and to generalize, he pretty much says, "Now what are you going to do about it?"

I like Dr. Phil. Not because he's on television. Not because he's successful, but because of why he's successful. He reminds me of Mom and Dad. "So you have no arms? Now what are you going to do about it?"

For some people who have suffered the reality of life's cruelty, those words can seem not only insensitive but truly insulting. "Now what are you going to do about it?" That's a good question.

I need you to know that there were times when having no arms wasn't easy. I have been stared at every single day of my life. Imagine that. Even simple math tells me that is over sixteen thousand times – if I only had one stare a day. I get much more. Going to school seemed a victory, but there were countless times it felt like a defeat. True, I did have friends, but every school has bullies. Some people talk about bullies these days as if they're a new thing – not even close. In fact, I would suggest, at least now we're addressing it. Then, it was ignored. As well meaning and caring as school officials were, they turned their back. I got laughed at, mocked, called names, and even beat up a couple of times. That expression, 'Sticks and stones can break my bones, but names can never hurt me' – I'd love to meet the idiot that dreamed that up. Trust me. Cuts heal. Bruises heal. But insults go deeper, to a place that is the essence of victimhood: the soul.

For me, the biggest hurt came from exclusion. I clearly remember the progression. Some schoolyard games I couldn't play, but Mrs. Plosz, my grade one teacher, for example, would improvise so I could play dodge ball. You aren't supposed to kick the ball, but for the sake of being able to take part, I was allowed. I could play soccer. Probably one of my first jokes about myself was I had the advantage because I never got a penalty for touching the ball with my hands (ha!). For the first few years of school I was always included in recess games, but somewhere around ten years old, and almost within a twenty-four hour period, I wasn't. It was as if the playground had elected a new leader, and one of his first acts was to declare *the freak without arms was uncool!* It's as if they had a secret meeting. It was unsettling. I didn't even do anything to anyone. So it began.

Imagine sitting against the wall of the school, watching all the people who used to be your friends and now weren't. I didn't know I wasn't alone. That's one of life's ironies. People who feel alienated because of indifference feel alone. The reality is there are tons of people feeling alone at the same time. Finding them is the trick. Yet, alone I was. My best friend, Pete, had moved. School was becoming tougher to go to every day. Don't get me wrong. Not *everybody* hated me, but on the playground, like life, people seemed hypnotized by what's *in*. Must wear what's *in*. Must go to what's *in*. Must be seen with who's *in*. It mystifies me to this day.

Looking back now, I can't blame everybody. I must accept some, if not much, of the responsibility for being sucked into it. I knew better. Heck, when I was four or five, and somebody at the playground beside St. Al's would make fun of me, I'd throw rocks at them. Okay, not a recommended behavior. I'm not proud of it, but I did it just the same. Seriously, what do little kids do when someone calls them a name? "I know you are, but what am I?" They deal with. I dealt with it. So what happens? What happens is what happened to me.

It occurred to me there are two groups in society who generally live with an *I Don't Care* kind of attitude: little kids and seniors. What happens to the big chunk in the middle? My theory is that when you're little, you're uninformed, and ignorance is bliss. When you're old, you've learned enough to know that most stuff doesn't matter. They say *life is about the journey.* If that's true, then a bunch of people, me included, take a few too many detours down the wrong roads. Even though lots of others show us the right map, we ignore it and go ahead anyway.

Mom and Dad told me I was a blessing. For a long time, I listened. Then, I stopped listening to them and started listening to myself. I had proof. I'm not special. I'm different. Check out my place on the school wall if you want your own evidence.

So you see, my idealistic approach to life hasn't always been the case. I hadn't even gotten to my teen years yet. I felt sorry for myself. I was confused, hurt, and alone. I felt the pain of something I certainly did not ask for. I asked 'why me?' I felt like a victim a lot of times. It was real. What didn't help was most of society saw people like me as a *victim*, too.

Now, I'm past forty. I'm okay with that, mostly because I know my own truth. Yet, I have met so many people with so-called disabilities who feel like victims. One of the problems with feeling victimized is that it happens twice. First, when it really occurs, and second, when we do it to ourselves. I always tell people that feeling sorry for yourself might be worse than what happened in the first place. Learning how to move forward is vital. We only get one life. Although some may feel cheated, it's still only one. What we do with it is what counts. Call me Dr. Al.

Kids often ask me if I can ride a bike. The answer is no, not a standard bicycle. Many go on to say they can ride *their* bikes without their hands, to which I pose my own question, why would you do something so dangerous? As much as I wanted to, I didn't ride a bicycle, but I had my own ride when I was young, and I loved it…a lot.

There were a lot of kids my age in the neighborhood. Most of us knew each other since we were toddlers together. I was comfortable and accepted among this group. There were four of us that hung around together, almost exclusively. When you saw one, you almost always saw the other three.

The first ride I started out with was a small pedal tractor. As I got older, I graduated to a tricycle. We have great home movies of "the gang" riding in a parade down the sidewalk on Fifth Avenue North in Yorkton. The four of us had the biggest smiles, oblivious to any differences we may have possessed. We were friends, and we were cruising!

As a child, Yorkton seemed huge to me. It wasn't very big, however. Even today, the population is just over seventeen thousand. One of the highlights for me was the Summer Fair and Exhibition. I have a distinct memory of the fair during the summer of 1970. That year, kids could enter their own floats in the Kiddies Day Parade. The floats could be anything mobile: bikes, wagons, and even tricycles – no in-line skates or scooters back in those days. The deal was you could decorate your unit and show up at the fire hall on the day of the parade, which was also the first day of the fair. If you made it all the way to the fairgrounds, you got in for free.

My parents decided that at ten years old, I was old enough to participate in this exciting event. My only problem was how I would decorate my wheeled unit. Our family was not well off, although we did not lack any of the necessities of life. However, my parents had lived through the Depression, so they were thrifty, to say the least. When I asked for some money to buy the coveted streamers and maybe even a bell, their response was "streamers and adornments would cost more than the entry fee for the fair." They were also very practical, which really didn't help my situation. I didn't usually beg or pester my parents for money or things, but this was very important to me. To get me to stop pestering them, I received the patented parent answer, "We'll see what happens when the time comes."

You already know that I don't ride a bicycle, so what exactly were the decorations for? It was a tricycle. I was almost ten years old, and I still rode a tricycle. It had been modified by my multi-skilled father. It was bigger and stronger and even included the 1970s requisite banana seat *and* sissy-bar (either you get that or you don't). Plus, it was my *bike* and all my friends were okay with that. I loved my tricycle. It just made sense to call it *my bike*. So when my friends and I got together, we went *biking*.

As the days wore on and the parade date approached, I still had no streamers, no bell, no decorations of any kind, and no hope on the horizon. To make matters worse, I discovered that my closest friends were going to be away. I would be entering the parade alone, that is, if I ever got any decorations to enter the parade myself. Suddenly, it was the day before the parade, still no decorations, so obviously, no parade participation.

To my surprise, and at first delight, Dad came home from work with a big grin and something rolled up under his arm. "Well, you are going to get to enter that parade. Here are your decorations!"

I was taught to be appreciative of all gifts because, as they say, "It's the thought that counts." But I knew there was no bell in there, and it didn't look like streamers to me. I was cautiously optimistic.

He unrolled the bundle under his arm and excitedly explained his idea. Mr. Mickelson (Dad's boss) gave him two posters of International Harvester trucks. "What we're going to do is tape one poster to each side of your bike. You can also wear this." At which point, he pulled an I-H cap from the back pocket of his coveralls. "You'll be *Truckerboy*!"

I tried to show my appreciation, but he must have noticed the look of dismay (if not horror) on my face. "Anyone can go to the Co-op store and buy overpriced bangles you'll use once and throw away. Where's the originality in that? You want to be different, stand out, right? I guarantee son, there won't be another one of these. I wouldn't be surprised if you even win a prize for originality and the best part…it didn't cost a cent."

When people say I was lucky to have my parents, I wholeheartedly agree…now. I suppose he was trying his best. I have no doubt he meant well, and certainly, his objective was to help, not humiliate me, but *Truckerboy?* This was definitely not what I had in mind. I certainly didn't need any more help standing out or being different. I could do that all on my own without even trying. What I wanted was to be like every other ten year old. I wanted to be cool!

It soon occurred to me that the options were pretty simple. Enter the parade as Yorkton's newest superhero or not enter the parade at all. I loved my tricycle, and I wanted to be in the parade, so *Truckerboy* it was.

I hardly slept that night. The concern over my decorations overshadowed my chance to ride in my first parade. I was up very early, and even though the parade didn't start until 10:00, I was there by 8:30. The only people already there were the firefighters who volunteered to help organize the start. Since their truck would lead the parade, it added to the excitement. They had drawn lines and numbers on the pavement in chalk. All of the participating children were instructed to line up behind the number corresponding with their age. I was the first to line up behind the ten.

The firefighters were very nice to me and even complimented me on my *float.* They were curious how I steered without hands, so I showed them. I just turned my legs with my feet on the pedals and because I rode every chance I could, I had perfected it. This was actually working out pretty well. Maybe it wouldn't be so bad. Other kids, most of them younger, started showing up. Several young riders had colorful ribbons and streamers on their tricycles, along with some older kids with nice bikes sporting pretty much the same streamers, ribbons, and bells. There was a very young girl with a dressed-up wagon with even an obedient small dog along for the ride, which wore corresponding colored ribbons. But it seemed Dad was right. My design *was* unique, and it seemed I would attract the much-desired attention a parade commands.

About ten minutes before the start, with well over a hundred kids lined up, a couple of very loud boys with flashy new bikes and matching cool clothes barged into the front of the twelve-year-old row. They seemed bent on disrupting things and ignored the complaints from those at the front who had arrived early. Bullies! They were two rows away. Maybe they wouldn't notice me. The problem was I was at the front of my line in what seemed a prime spot for the start of the parade. It also put me in the line of fire.

It didn't take long for them to notice me and even less time to point me out to each other. It seemed too much to hope they might have been impressed by my decorations. I didn't know these boys or anyone else near me. I could see what was coming, and it was not going to be pretty.

First they started to laugh. It was likely they were making fun of my having no arms. I was used to that. It was also likely they were making fun of my decorations, but since the firefighters approved, I really didn't care that much. They did throw the predictable line at me: "Where's your arms? Forget 'em at home?" Ha, ha…how original. They instead hurled another no-brainer: "Where'd you get your decorations? At Zig's?" Yorkton was located at the crossroads of four highways, and Zig's was a well-known local truck stop.

Then I heard it, the one that hit home, "Shouldn't you be in the five-year-old row? That's where the tricycles are. Or maybe you are five and you just grew bigger instead of growing arms!"

I knew everyone, and I mean everyone, around me were on bicycles. The nearest tricycle was five rows and fifty feet away, but until that minute it hadn't mattered. Then it happened, just because that is the way human nature works, others joined in the taunts. Nobody stuck up for me. If there was an adult around, they either didn't notice or chose not to say anything. The firefighters were in their truck ready to go. My best friends were away, and my parents weren't even there. Dad was at work, and Mom was already at the fairgrounds volunteering in the United Church Women's concession stand. The plan was for me to meet up with her there. I was not only alone, I was all alone.

I'd been made fun of before. I was used to being stared at. This wasn't the first time I had been laughed at, picked on, called names, and made to feel like a freak. But no matter how many times it happened before, it still hurt. I never got used to it.

For the first time, I considered that maybe they were right. Maybe my parents were wrong. Maybe all their friends, all my friends, all of them were just patronizing me. Maybe they all felt sorry for me and kept it to themselves. And then I started feeling sorry for myself.

With two minutes before the parade began, I crossed the line with my tricycle, turned away from the unrelenting crowd, and raced away as fast as I could. I raced straight home, fifteen blocks. I couldn't even see where I was going because the tears filled my eyes and streamed down my face, just like the baby those kids said I was. It was like in the old Western movies, where the horse carries its lifeless passenger back to the ranch. I may have been alive, but in another first, I wished I wasn't.

When I reached our yard, I ripped the posters from my tricycle, tore them to shreds, and threw them and the I-H cap in the trash. I kicked over what, moments before, was my most prized possession but was now a dreadful symbol of what I really was. I was a troll, a mutant, a disgusting reminder of what happens when God makes a mistake. And even though I had been reminded over and over again that God doesn't make mistakes, it had to be lie. I was the proof.

It is truly tragic that in these supposed enlightened days of the twenty-first century, we hear of young people taking their own lives to stop the bullying, harassment, and the torment of others. Or worse, some of them take the lives of others they feel have harmed them in some way. You think it should be easy to just ignore the relentless torture of words and exclusion, blank it out like it doesn't exist. But it does exist. The pain exists, and at that moment, you think it will always exist until the end of time.

It did take me a long time to get over that day. In some respects, I don't think I have ever totally recovered. I know I wasn't the same after that. I never attempted to ride in another parade. Soon I was riding my bike and hanging out with my friends less and less.

Bullying seems to be one of the most talked about issues in our schools today, but it isn't just today and it isn't just in schools. Bullying has been around for a long time in our homes, schools and workplaces. Not unlike the cycle of violence against women, by educating ourselves and our children about the effects of bullying, we can stop the cycle and make things better for those who come after us.

I read a study a while ago that said kids at the age of ten start to doubt and question the things their parents teach them. Not as teenagers – by then they have momentum. I was ten when I started to doubt my parents, my teachers, and even my friends. I was starting to believe all the negative things I heard and questioned everything else.

Luckily, I had the balance of some kind and caring people entering into my life that helped me find and keep that belief in myself once more, but these lessons were hard to learn.

chapter ten

everyone has value

There is, of course, a huge difference between speaking and writing, the least of which is that being good at one doesn't mean you're good at the other. Another thing, unless it's recorded, a speech is heard and *essentially* disappears. I wrote my *Laws* in 2003. The first version of the "V" was *Virtue versus Victim*. I borrowed it from an elementary school that invited me to speak during *Respect Month*. Great school. It had a different theme every month. The focus was on human, not scholastic, elements. Imagine that. A school believing there is more to an education than the three R's. They even had a mission statement. It was a cool place. One of the beliefs they wanted me to discuss was the idea that kids need to see their virtues rather than feel like victims. By the way, this was a nice school in a very tough neighborhood. Most of the students were very poor financially. I liked it, so I borrowed it and wrote a paragraph about what it meant.

Over time, I still liked it, but on paper, it's a bit unclear without the paragraph. So I changed the words but believe the meaning is the same. *Everyone has value. Finding it – that's the trick!*

Going to school was, at first, as good as it could get, although nothing philosophical was happening for me. I was part of the whole nerdy bunch. If the game at recess was dodge ball, I played dodge ball. If it was soccer, I played soccer. If it was hanging on the monkey bars, I played soccer. Inclusion through patronization was a good thing. This was also a very different time. Parents weren't over-programming their kids from age three, and the minivan hadn't been invented yet. Whatever *activity* one was supposed to immerse oneself into started much later when I was a kid.

Look, don't get me wrong. I think we need to have our kids do activities. There probably isn't anything life-altering starting them young, but honestly, as parents, when we enroll them into ballet, sports, pageants, etc. is it for them or us? Kids' brains are going through more stimulation. How about some quiet time, without activities, television, video games, or makeover parties for seven year olds?

About the minivan and over-programming, please don't take it personal, but I need to explain. Each school day, four times a day, we get to watch the minivan parade of kids being driven to and from school. But the bottom line is, today's parents coddle their kids. Not all, but from my viewpoint, a lot. Kids need to be less tethered to their parents.

I was remarkably lucky in that my parents came to own a dinky little cabin at a place few have heard of: Crystal Lake, Saskatchewan. Unlike my brothers, I got to spend summers there. Although I'm biased, it is a magical place.

For me, it was all about the tether. At Crystal, there wasn't one. I'd be away from Mom (Dad only came out on weekends) all day, well, except for lunch and maybe snacks. At Crystal, I had no fear. Boy was there a lot to explore! I learned to fish, throw and skip stones, and swim (Dad pushed me off our dock when I was 12 – on purpose). The list is endless. I also had the extreme good fortune of getting to know many other people who spent their time there. I felt truly special, not different.

Back on the playground, my inclusion in the nerd bunch was changing with age. By grade four, I wasn't included as much, and the cliques were beginning to form. It seemed kind of obvious I wasn't destined for high-performance athletics. As it turned out, both dynamics were about to clash in a most unexpected place.

I got detention. I was in trouble because an older kid had made fun of me. Instead of running to the principal, the human rights commission, or a personal injury lawyer, I threw a rock at him. Hit him right in the forehead, actually. It was a great shot. It shut him up all right, but I got detention. I had to clean all the blackboards, no mean feat without arms. I actually had to stand on a stool with one foot and clean with the other. When I was done, the school was empty, except for the janitor, Mr. Persyck.

I think janitors are one of the most unappreciated professions, especially school janitors, and even more, junior high and high school janitors who have to clean up after lazy kids. I have a suggestion for you after you're done this book. The next time you see a janitor, give them a hug. Okay? Look, I've seen lots of janitors. Being that close to them may not be overly motivating, but trust me, they deserve it.

Mr. Persyck was a great janitor and a real tall (he got shorter as we got older) "Farmer Bob" kind of guy. He had a son named Leroy (is that a great name?) who used to help his dad once in awhile. Leroy ended up as the principal of St. Al's...cool, huh?

Anyway, I was slinking home, pretty confused, and as I walked past the music room, it was uncharacteristically unlocked. Inside were all kinds of musical temptations, but what caught my eye was the piano. I'd seen it lots of times and sang along with it countless times, but I'd never been allowed to touch it. I'd never played a piano, period. I had probably banged on it a few times as a small child but never played one. It was still probably off limits, but I've always believed there are too many rules. So I snuck in, pulled out the bench, opened the key cover, and pretty much stared at it at first.

I have always had to learn things twice in a way. Once like everyone else and then once my way. I was aware of piano stuff, but I was entering new terrain here. It would be real dramatic if the first time I played I was like some child prodigy, and by ear, cranked out Beethoven's Fifth, but I had to settle for "Chopsticks." It sounded pretty good, well, as good as Chopsticks can sound after round one. I began round two (second verse, same as the first) and about halfway through, my virtuosity was rudely interrupted by a shrieking voice that sounded all too familiar.

St. Al's was a Catholic school. We had a couple of nuns in residence (not literally but close) and one was Sister Theresa. With respect, to us she looked at least a hundred but was probably closer to seventy years old. Sister Theresa had a bit of an edge to her, and it took milliseconds to know who was behind me.

"Alvin! What are you doing?"

"Nothing," was my reply. Hey, I was ten.

"Nothing? It doesn't look like nothing! How did you get in here?"

"The door was open, so I just sort of walked in."

"Did you get permission to play the piano?"

"Not exactly."

"Not exactly?" She turned down the volume a bit and asked me what I was playing. I didn't know what it was called and told her that. Then came a big surprise.

"Play it again." I wanted to say, "what?" but I'd heard her okay. So I did. Just like in *Casablanca* with Humphry Bogart, I played it again. This time she didn't scream. She actually got real quiet and walked toward me. Then she hugged me from behind (back when teachers could hug kids without lawsuits) and to put the finishing touch on a moment one might describe as unpredictable – she kissed my forehead and said, "You truly are a gift from God."

Wow. She must have known, being a nun and all. It was nice to be a gift, especially since I'd felt like more of a curse than a blessing…a lot more. This feeling wasn't new. I had felt special a lot. Mom was particularly good at it, but moms are supposed to do that. Sister Theresa didn't have to say that, but she did.

Do you realize how many opportunities a person has to make, or break, another person's day? When I'm asked about what lessons I've learned in life, one of them is about the oldest lesson there is and one of the first we're all taught: *The Golden Rule! Do unto others as you might have them do unto you.* I cannot believe how simple this stuff is and how hard we make it.

Here's a list of the people I make a point of being nice to every chance I get:

- The maid at my hotel and the person who brings me room service
- The one who works behind the counter at everything
- The garbage collector, the postal carrier, and the courier
- The lady who cleans my teeth (especially her – what a gross job)
- My doctor and every nurse I've ever met
- Teachers (actually I'd give most of them a million dollars each just because they don't get even close to the respect they deserve, but since I don't have a million dollars, I'll let Bill Gates and his conscience give it a go)
- My neighbors, even though I don't know them as well as I should

- Anyone behind the glass doors at drive-thru restaurants for taking the money from my foot and not grossing out
- The guy who fixes my car
- The lady who alters my clothes so I can dress myself
- The people who sell me my clothes that cost a lot but I have to have so I can do my job and especially the people that sell shoes (another gross job)
- The people who clean rental cars, drive them, park them, check them in, and especially the ones who give me the car in the first place (It still amazes me they give me the keys to a forty thousand dollar car without flinching, even the bag in England who wouldn't give me a car because she had no class whatsoever.)
- Airline check-in and gate agents, the people who clean the plane (gross), flight attendants and pilots (especially pilots for obvious reasons)
- Grocery store clerks, stockers (not the other kind), and the ones who put my stuff in the bags and almost never put the heavy stuff on the eggs
- People that rent me movies (I watch a lot of them), take my tickets at the theater, and those who give me the pathetically overpriced popcorn that smells so good you'll pay anything for it
- Moms with babies who cry on airplanes because their ears hurt or kids with moms who cry because they're having a bad day
- People who get airsick and have to use those ridiculously small bags for relief (they are hard to be nice to because that smell is not pleasant)
- Old people…always!
- Kids who stare and blurt out, "That guy has no arms!" and even adults who do the same but should know better.
- Well, I suppose just about anyone and everyone because I truly believe in the adage, 'do unto others.'

Everyone has value. Sister Theresa taught me that!

chapter eleven
my symphony

It was just "Chopsticks," but it was my symphony. I don't know what was the bigger highlight, the piano or Sister Theresa's proclamation. All I remember is my detention was over for the day. All I wanted to do was race home and tell Mom what had happened. I also remember that Mom was pretty calm about it all. You are probably noticing a pattern forming. I suppose a person's nature comes into play here. Mom's was about as balanced as they come. I really don't know how she did it. She also knew when something had emerged out of the ordinary, and before I knew it, I was on the *Yorkton Elderly Women's Tea Party Circuit!* We didn't own a piano, but a lot of Mom's friends did. Whenever the opportunity arose, I would play Chopsticks for them.

As I have already alluded to, much of what I have become I give credit to my surroundings. I am so curious about it, though. How did this all happen? Like in the Bogart movie again, 'Of all the gin joints,' how did I land in this life? *It was meant to be.* I kind of like that. One thing I would say is I was very fortunate, considering all of the other alternatives. In retrospect, this was a great time in my life. Maybe I was naive. Ignorance can be a good thing. I would play my little one-song-symphony. It wasn't very good, but the grandmas would clap and cheer. I almost always got milk and cookies and hugs and kisses. How it made me feel was powerful. Honestly, I probably expected it because my mom's friends, heck, my parents' friends, were so awesome. I suppose that considering what my folks were like, their having great friends shouldn't come as such a surprise. The fact was, their life couldn't have fit any better with mine, but like all real life, it usually changes the further you travel from the shelter of your loved ones.

Obviously, at ten years old, I wasn't about to head out on a world tour. I played for a lady one day, and although she was also a grandma, something wasn't the same. I couldn't nail it down, but it was a *feeling*.

After my trademark tune, we went to the kitchen, presumably for milk and cookies. Instead, she said, "Show me your foot!"

Odd request. I held it up, and she looked, but didn't touch, and said, "Have you ever noticed how short your toes are?"

You know, I hadn't and told her so. I rather loved my feet. She then launched into an interesting little commentary.

"I'm a piano teacher, Alvin. Your mother has asked me to give you lessons." I couldn't believe my ears.

"You know, I've been teachings kids to play piano for twenty-seven years. In all that time, I have never seen anyone like you. You are a remarkable boy. Your mom is a remarkable woman. There isn't anything that would make me happier than to teach you." (Cool!)

"But I can't. Nothing personal, but by looking at your toes, I can tell that no amount of lessons would ever help, and it isn't your fault. You didn't ask to be born this way right?" (Duh!)

"You didn't ask to have short toes, and you certainly didn't ask for this, but just like some people are geniuses and others aren't, some people are athletic and others aren't, some people are beautiful and others aren't, some people were meant to play the piano – but not you. Honestly, I mean no offence. My advice, for what it's worth, is that you wear those artificial arms the doctors gave you, and maybe, just maybe, you can use those to play the piano someday."

I need to tell you that what that lady said was way less than the worst thing I'd heard. That day was tiny when compared with countless big, bad days. Yet, in a way, it was a very profound day. Of course, I didn't know it then. Don't get me wrong. That day hurt – a lot! What seemed to hurt the most was I just didn't want to play the piano anymore. I guess she took away the joy. But let's look at it another way.

How about the notion that I *allowed* her to take the joy away? Truth be known, she was probably right. From a pure state of mind, what she said was accurate. I still have short toes. Although constantly being compared to fingers by those amazed by me, they're still toes. It's straight physics. Cause and effect. The design of fingers proves much more efficient for the physical action required to strike a piano key, or more importantly, multiple keys. Taken in progression, they form the music that emanates from the further action of the key moving the hammer, which then strikes the corresponding string, which causes a vibration of varying degree dependent on the energy created by the strike of the hammer, which then exits the piano body through sound vibration, which eventually enters the human ear drum causing it to vibrate, which is then decoded through the miracles of the human brain allowing us to enjoy the music.

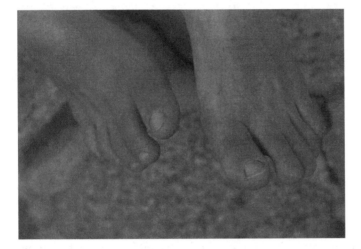

She had a point. Toes aren't complex enough. Pianos were meant to be played with fingers. Thus the design. Then, as now, there is probably a limited market for pianos being played with one's toes. Silly, really, if you think about my dream. Probably as silly as the ludicrous notion that a composer could be deaf!

chapter twelve

play ball!

I have a quick question. How are you doing? Pretty dumb thing to ask, considering you can't answer me. This writing thing is weird for a speaker. I guess what I'm hoping is that you are connecting my stories with your life. I often make a reference to *Biography* on the A&E Network in North America. Its tag line is, "Every life has a story." I couldn't agree more. Please never underestimate the stories of your life. Do you have some favorites? This story is one of mine. In fact, it's probably in the top five.

It was spring, and that meant many things in Saskatchewan. I was just glad the snow usually left by Easter, and I could shed some clothes. I hate clothes. Actually, I dislike the act of dressing myself, as it is a tad complicated. Nothing was different about spring until one day.

Behind St. Al's, there was a baseball diamond. I had played there quite a bit. I used to play imaginary baseball once in a while, mostly running the bases and sliding. It may have been wishing just to get dirty as opposed to the actual game itself. One day after school, there were tryouts for Little League. The team that called St. Al's diamond home was the *Dunlop Dun-Rites*. They were sponsored by a tire dealership and coached by one of its employees. In many ways, it was a community team. All the self-esteem cops were yet to be born, so you had to *make* the team.

As you may recall, I went to St. Al's school, but many of my neighborhood friends went to the public school. They still included me in games like *kick-the-can* and *hide-and-seek*. That day, they invited me to come to the tryouts. I had no illusions. I was no dummy. I wasn't going to try out, but simply tag along. I suppose somewhere inside of me, I secretly wished I could play baseball. I know, even as a middle-aged man, I still *wish* I could do some things. It is tough, but you just deal with it.

So on went the try-out. All my friends made the Dun-Rites. I enjoyed just being there, but after everyone was gone, I felt an urge to play another little imaginary game. I pretended it was game seven of the World Series. The score was tied at the top of the ninth with the bases loaded for the bad guys and nobody out. I was called in from the bullpen. My job was simple. Don't let them score. By the way, I have seen home movies of me pretending to golf, pretending to curl, and pretending to play ball; I look pathetic because I'm also pretending to have arms too! But, there I was, on the mound, the World Series on the line. I was getting the signs, chewing, spitting, and doing that other thing baseball players do that involves protective equipment. I started hurling the heat. Nine pitches later, I struck out the side.

Then it was my turn at the plate. Even though I was a pitcher, I planned on a home run to win everything. My hit just about cleared the wall, but instead it hit it and bounced back, giving me a chance for the inside-the-park homer. At this point, I was actually running myself. As I took the big turn at third, I knew the play would be at the plate. The catcher had the ball and was blocking the plate. I knew I had to make the big play, so I slid…feet first, of course (I wasn't stupid), and aimed my right foot at his glove holding the ball. Miracles do happen. The ball popped loose. As it fell to the ground, I slid across the plate, and just like that, I won the World Series!

It was great. The fans went nuts. The band started to play. Flashbulbs went off. My teammates flooded the field, picked me up, and carried me around the diamond, while they prepared the stage for the trophy presentation. I was a true hero. I had accomplished the greatest athletic dream and won the big one for my team. I'd be famous. I'd probably go to Cooperstown. I'd even get a huge ring. It was the most amazing moment until…

Did you ever get caught playing imaginary games when you were young? It's embarrassing. As I slid for real, I heard clapping – for real. There was guy standing fifty feet away, clapping. All I wanted to do was run home, but he was blocking the way.

"I want to talk to you!" he hollered and sort of frightened me.
"Do you know who I am?" he said as he approached me.

"No."

"My name is Mr. White. I'm the coach of the Dun-Rites."

"Oh yea, I've seen you before."

"I've seen you too. You live around here, right?"

"Across the street; am I in trouble?"

"No, I just want to talk to you." Then he just stood there. He was carrying a gym bag. He put it down, put his hands on his hips, and said, "You love baseball, don't you?"

"Yea," I replied. Then he was quiet again. He bent over, opened up his bag, and pulled out a black and orange jersey.

He held it up and asked, "Do you know what this is?"

I knew right away. "That's a Dun-Rites jersey."

"Would you like it?"

Would I like it? I was only ten years old, but I had one thing figured out, if you're handicapped and you play your cards right, you can get lots of free stuff.

I was uncharacteristically silent, but my face must have spoken because he then said, "You can have it on one condition. You have to get your mom to fix up the sleeves and you have to be here at 5:00 on Tuesday."

"For what?" I asked.

"Practice!"

"For what?"

What he said next kind of came under the heading of *am I hearing things?*

"I want you on my team!"

I sometimes wonder what my face looked like then. I know Mr. White smiled, but if he smiled for long, I don't know because I grabbed the jersey under my chin. I said I'd be there and raced home faster than I'd ever ran.

Please remember, I had a good life. Truthfully, I hadn't lain awake nights dreaming of playing baseball. What I did dream about was a common dream for so many people – to be on a team. Or perhaps more important, to be included as opposed to being excluded. I believe this subject is one of the most profound of human dynamics, so important that one might write a book about this alone (I'm sure someone has). I mention this because I don't want to simply brush over it by it being only one chapter. Yet I don't want to get too bogged down here because there are many more of these dynamics I want to explore.

I raced into the house screaming for my mom. She must have thought I was hurt because she came rushing up from the basement and asked me if I was okay. I didn't answer. I just gave her the jersey and exclaimed, "I'm a *Dun-Rite!*"

"You're a what?"

"I'm on the team."

"What team?"

"The baseball team."

Mom gave me one of those mom looks and said, "Did you steal this?"

"No Mom. Mr. White gave it to me. He told me to be at the diamond on Tuesday for our first practice."

"What position are you supposed to be playing?"

The Dun-Rites 1969
Alvin, front row, second from the left

That was a good question. I replied, "He didn't say." And then I started thinking about the obvious. Mom asked me to explain, so I told her about the tryouts, my little game, and the conversation with the coach. She got tears in her eyes. Then she hugged me and told me to do my homework. Back to reality.

I tried to concentrate on my homework, but I couldn't get it out of my mind. The following days took forever, but Tuesday eventually showed up. I even wore my jersey to practice only to find out they were for games only. So I took it off and sat on the grass with my teammates (what a cool thing to be able to say). The coach gave us a little talk about his expectations, stressing for us to have fun but also remember we were a team. The most important thing was to respect each other because some would be better at the game than others. That's the way life works.

I honestly had a piano-teacher flashback. Remember the complications of human dynamics? I didn't have much time to get too deep because it was time to run. That, I could do. We all ran around the entire field, twice. Then we did a bunch of stuff the coach called calisthenics. I could have cared less what it was called. All I knew was this wasn't what I thought it was going to be. After we were mostly worn out, the coach told us that nobody would play just one position, and everyone would play. At that point, seriously, everybody looked at me.

I looked at me too. The coach told everyone to grab their gloves (at that point it occurred to me I didn't bring or own a baseball glove) and start playing catch. He numbered everyone, who then paired up and started the exercise. Coach White took me aside, and with such kindness in his eyes, explained my role.

I can't remember his exact words, but I will never forget the message. I was going to be the team's designated pinch runner. Most of my responsibilities would occur during practices, when I would help with infield drills. Because everyone would play during games, I would too. How that would happen was unclear, but I didn't care. Coach White made me feel a part of the team, and that, I could identify with.

We had one more practice before our home opener a few days later. I wore my jersey, and my pride meter hit a new high. Dad even came home early from work, something he never did. He sat beside my mom in a couple of lawn chairs. When our team took the field for the first inning, all the other parents cheered, and as their noise was dying down, Dad shouted, "Way to go, son!"

I was on the bench. As much as I was usually proud of my parents, I turned around and said to Dad, who wasn't far away, "I'm on the bench!"

"Way to go anyway!"

When is the last time you cheered for your kid being on the bench or getting a "C" instead of a "D?" We can't all be the best. We are who we are.

I still had a blast that day. In the fourth inning, I found out how I would participate. It may appear patronizing, but what happened was someone on our team who had already batted twice would hit for me. I would stand next to home plate. If the batter connected, I would run as if it were my at-bat. I even scored in my first at-bat. We won the game, too, although we won by a lot so my run wasn't pivotal. That spring was about the best season I ever had. There wasn't a championship. We won more than we lost, but that didn't matter.

Imagine, yet again, how many messages one might take away from this story. I want to focus on one. My relationship with Ken White was baseball. I didn't really know him but understood he was a lot like my dad. He worked a blue-collar job. He put tires on rims for a living (amongst other things I'm sure), and I wonder sometimes if he felt his life was somehow unimportant. He wasn't the mayor. He didn't cure cancer. He never won the Nobel Peace Prize. But for one baseball season, he gave a little armless boy an experience that he has *never* forgotten.

Too many people think that making a difference is beyond their "pay-scale." Little League anything is always looking for volunteers to help kids play games. If you feel your life is missing something, give something that is priceless: your time. Too many kids go through their whole childhood without experiencing the joy of organized sports. Is winning nice? Sure. It's why we keep score. But in the grand scheme of things, wearing a jersey, sitting on a bench, and being part of a team is something that is also priceless. Thanks Coach White! Thanks for asking me to play.

section IV - imagination

is for imagination

*Imagination is the key that unlocks the
power of potential. It is not owned by the
young, but they are best at using it. It defines
the difference between obstacles and possibilities.
Imagination leads to dreams, and
dreams make life worth living.
Dreams can come true...this I know.*

chapter thirteen

christmas in may

The school year of 1970-71 would end up being quite the year. In grade four, I had Sister Ignacious for my teacher. She was gentle, kind, quiet, and compassionate. Grade five, I had Mr. Herauf. He was not Sister Ignacious in any way at all. He lived for discipline and had high expectations. He was *not* warm and fuzzy. As if that wasn't bad enough, he knew something I thought only I knew. Well, in truth, not just me. I suppose most of my friends at the rehab hospitals knew it too, but he was the first person I met in Yorkton who knew it. It was supposed to be just my secret. Mr. Herauf had only one arm. He lost his other in an accident as a child, and it seemed at first, he was a tad bitter about it. In fact, my first impression of the man was that he was just plain mean.

What's the secret? You see, many handicapped people, especially those born that way, learn to work the system. I couldn't work it at home, but I could at school. I even worked it in the hospitals, on occasion. It may not be something to be proud of, but you've got to do what you've got to do. By the system, I mean, getting away with stuff. Sister Ignacious was almost the nicest person I ever met. As much as   I hate to admit it because I'm sure God will read this, I worked her too. I would pretend I couldn't do something in class, couldn't do a homework assignment, or couldn't participate in a project because I had no arms. I learned that being handicapped could be a good thing. It gets you moved to the front of the line, the front row of the show, and the best seat in a restaurant. You get the idea. It's like people want to do stuff for you just because you're handicapped. It's a very kind gesture, and in some respects, genuinely appreciated, but in some other respects, it's pretty pathetic when people "use" it.

Mr. Herauf knew my secret. It seemed, with him, the free ride was over. In truth, I needed Mr. Herauf. I was learning about the dark side of the handicap game, and for lack of a better expression, he called me on it. I was getting lazy, so he gave me extra homework. I was getting mouthy, so he gave me extra detention. He even made me rewrite my entire science notebook over the Christmas holidays because it was messy and he couldn't read it. See what I mean? Mean! He actually had high expectations of me. I didn't like him much then. Looking back, I owe him more than I can describe because, although the next segment is about someone else, it really was possible because of Mr. Herauf. His relentless discipline made me a better student and allowed me to excel on an exam that would change the course of my life.

In early 1971, my mom got a phone call that went like this:

"Hello."

"Mrs. Law? My name is Blaine McClary. I'm the band director for the Yorkton City Band Program. Do you have a son named Alvin?"

"Yes."

"Does Alvin have a talent for music that you're aware of?"

"You know, he used to play piano a bit, but he quit one day. We're not sure why. Why are you calling?"

"Mrs. Law, all fifth graders in Yorkton have to take a music aptitude test at school. Did you know about it?"

"No, we didn't know."

"Well Mrs. Law, I have some good news. Your son got ninety-six percent."

"Wow!"

"Yes and that's why I'm calling. We'd like to invite Alvin to join the band."

"Pardon me?"

"The school band, Mrs. Law. Do you think he would be interested?"

"Sorry, this is a bit of a surprise, but I'm sure he'd be interested. It might be a bit complicated."

"Complicated?"

"Yes. For example, what instrument did you have in mind?"

"Mrs. Law, we normally don't do this, but with that kind of talent, why don't you just bring your son to the high school and he can pick any instrument he wants."

Insert pause here.

"Mr. McClary, have you met Alvin?"

"No, I just have his phone number, why?"

"Sir, you should probably know that Alvin has no arms."

Silence and another pause.

"Hello? Mr. McClary, are you still there?"

"Mrs. Law, I didn't know that. Sorry to bother you, have a nice day."

Click. The phone went dead.

One might make several observations about humanity at this point, but just for fun, imagine you're the band director. You work in a relatively good-sized community for Saskatchewan. You have a fair sized band program and aren't exactly desperate for players. This was 1971. There weren't yet integration programs. In some places, the world was still dealing with letting black people drink at the same water fountains as whites. The issue of human rights was an interesting discussion at left wing political gatherings. I know I keep referring to the era, and I'm not simply reminiscing. I'm fascinated with how much change took place in the 1970s regarding the equality of people. How did it happen?

In my speeches, I ask my audience what they would do. Would you put a little armless kid in the band? There is the obvious, politically correct, right answer, but there wasn't such a thing as politically correct in 1971. Then there was honesty. Most people would probably just move on and not bother because even if you could figure out an instrument for the child to play, what would be the point? They couldn't contribute to the quality of the band's music; if anything, they would hold back the band and be an eyesore and a hassle. Sorry, I do get a wee bit cranky when I think of how things were and often still are. But if the injustices of the time make me cranky, the second part of this story makes me elated.

I can only speculate the reason, but a few weeks after his initial contact with my mom, the band director phoned back. I was never told of the first phone call because Mom had a way of moderating my *hope factor*. All I know is I came home from school in grade five and Mom had that look. The last time I got that look, I got those dorky artificial arms. She just seemed so excited. I couldn't imagine why, and then the words I will remember forever: "Alvin, great news. You're going to be in the band!"

The Beatles, Led Zeppelin, or if my dad had his way, Lawrence Welk? My mind was racing trying to imagine what I'd just heard. All I know is we got in the car and went to the almost new Yorkton Regional High School. On the way, Mom told me about the first telephone call, her keeping it from me, and her surprise that he didn't forget about me.

What fascinates me to this day is how clearly I remember the trip. One doesn't always register with clarity our daily events. The prospect of being in a band was cool, but it's not as if I was competing in the Olympics and had been preparing my whole life for that once-in-a-lifetime moment.

We met Mr. McClary at the front of the school, who then led

Blaine McClary

us to the vocational wing. With Dad being a mechanic, being around the trades was fine with me. Little did I know that the vocational wing was thought of a bit negatively in the school world. All I knew was this was a big school, and these classrooms were huge. The room we ended up in seemed as big as all of St. Al's. It was the room they taught construction and woodworking. There was wood everywhere plus circular saws, drill presses, sanding machines, and countless other construction paraphernalia. And there was sawdust. There is no smell like sawdust. Imagine this huge room almost two stories high, and in the middle of the room, a little wooden chair.

Standing by the chair were two teachers: the high school physics instructor and the woodworking teacher, whose name was Mr. Wood (I always thought that was cool). The chair itself looked funny. I guess it was a standard issue teacher's chair, but it didn't look very standard. The right arm had been removed and the left arm had a metal rod bolted to the side with a clamp welded to the top. There was another metal rod and clamp bolted to the back. On the floor beside the chair was a long black case with a small crown logo by the handle.

I guess you need to know I had no clue what was in that case. You also need to know I had been with my share of experts who had constructed things to assist me and pretty much every one had failed. These seemed like experts, but they were different somehow. I have often joked that Mr. McClary looked like Santa Claus. Well, this was May and there was no Christmas tree, but there was the same anticipation. What was in that case?

Mr. McClary asked me to sit in the chair, which I did. He knelt down and clicked open the clasps on the front of the black case, tilted the top back, and pulled out a shiny, silver colored brass horn. He placed it in the clamps on the chair and locked them down. He then pulled out a second piece, a long silver u-shaped tube, and connected it to the horn, tightening a ring, which made it…a trombone! A trombone? I didn't want to play trombone. Or did I? I was so confused. He then handed me what was described as a mouthpiece. It was heavy but very shiny. I held it in my toes. Now what?

Mr. McClary asked me to buzz my lips like him, and he buzzed. To be honest, I laughed. It sounded like a fart. All ten year olds laugh at farts, whether real or imitated by various body parts (I was always a little disappointed I couldn't do the armpit one). Mom gave me her *behave yourself* look and I stopped. Now, it was my turn. I buzzed my lips, it felt funny, and I almost laughed again, but Mom's *look* was not to be messed with. I then was instructed to buzz into the mouthpiece. It was really hard not to laugh. It sounded so weird. I was shown where to insert the mouthpiece and asked to buzz into the mouthpiece again. This time, I didn't laugh. It actually startled me. It startled everybody. It was loud. Mr. McClary didn't seem surprised, but he did smile and asked me if I could reach the slide with my right foot. I could. He showed me the lock and undid it, instructing me to hold the slide and then slowly move it back and forth. I did. He asked me to buzz into the mouthpiece and move the slide at the same time. When I did, it felt like nothing I had ever felt. Mr. McClary asked me to stop. I did. I will never forget that moment. You should have been there.

Mr. McClary smiled, and without any drama, proclaimed this would be what I would play in the band. Mom got tears in her eyes. The two other teachers seemed like they were going to dance together, and I just sat there. I could only think of one thing while they packed up the trombone, carried it and the chair to our car. While Mom drove home with a Cheshire cat grin, all I could think of was, "How am I going to march?"

chapter fourteen

start me up

In 1970, Mr. McClary, a complete stranger did something for me I believe played a huge role in making me the person I am today. I didn't know that when I was ten. All I remember was Mom lugging the chair, its metal braces, and the trombone case downstairs. She told me to set it up like at school. She went upstairs and left me alone with my new instrument. It's important to keep something in mind; this wasn't my dream. I'm not sure I even had one. Some people appear to be the epitome of dreams coming true.

For example, when I watch a hockey team win the Stanley Cup and when players are interviewed by the press, they passionately explain how it was their dream, since they were a little kid, to hoist Lord Stanley's mug over their head. I actually find myself crying. I don't even know these guys. What if, God forbid, they were jerks undeserving of such an honor, and here I was crying for them. I'm pretty sure that wasn't the case. It's just weird to be so emotional for someone I don't even know. It's probably envy, not so much for the trophy, but the feeling. Everyone wants to be a winner.

Believe it or not, I had never actually thought about a trombone. I imagined Elvis getting his first guitar, Joe Montana getting his first football, or Babe Ruth getting his first bat. I had a trombone. Maybe Glenn Miller felt something, but I felt confused. However, I had been given a job to do, so I opened up the case to set up my new instrument.

Actually, it was beautiful. The case was shiny and black on the outside and impeccable blue velvet on the inside. It covered the form fitting foam that held the bell and slide in two separate compartments. The brass was covered with a silver finish that gleamed from the velvet. I didn't want to touch it. I just stared and wondered why I felt so weird. Now, if this were a new set of golf clubs and someone had miraculously discovered a way for me to golf, I could be excited. But a trombone?

Yet, and please allow me this, I think I felt a hint, a hint of a dream. Honest. I know this was a long time ago, but while writing this book, I have focused deeply on my memories, both for the accuracy of the stories and for the emotions. Some memories are a bit fuzzy, but this one is as clear as a cold Saskatchewan winter morning. Something in the back of my mind told me this was a special moment, but the front of my mind was focused on something else. Why a trombone? Why not a guitar, or drums, or something remotely groovy (this was 1970)? Oh well, Dad had made me take tap dancing lessons. Maybe there was a pattern forming.

I reached down with my feet and gently pulled the main bell of the horn from its cushiony bed, as careful as I could. For the first of what would become thousands of times, I inserted it in the clamps. I made sure the screws were tight, then from the case, extracted the slide, fit it to the bell, and slowly turned the brass coupler until the slide was tight. I pulled out the mouthpiece. This was a very special moment. Just before placing it in the slide, I buzzed into it again just because I wanted to hear the fart noise again. Mom yelled my name from upstairs and the ceremony was complete. I had set up my instrument. It looked kind of goofy, but attractive at the same time, so I sat in the chair again, placed my lips to the mouthpiece, buzzed my lips, and the unmistakable blast of a large brass horn erupted from the bell.

You know, it was kind of neat. You made a noise at one end and a much bigger noise came out the other. I was ten. Ten year olds like noise, especially making it. Maybe this wouldn't be so bad. It was shiny, had moving parts, and came with a spray bottle, so you could squirt other musicians in band, I assumed. Most of the following weekend, I basically hung out in the basement trying to come up with new noises, while my parents brought almost everyone they knew downstairs for the tour. This seemed like a big deal.

The following Tuesday, after school, I had a house call. It wasn't from a doctor, but she was a miracle worker in her own right. I didn't know that at the time either.

I am so fascinated with human interaction that results in a positive story. Like any story, when it begins, you have no idea where it might lead and when it has a happy ending, you want to read it again. I love reliving my meeting Cindy Knapp.

Cindy Knapp was from Hastings, Nebraska and was in her first year of teaching beginner band in Yorkton. She spent busy days going from school to school helping new musicians. Her busiest time was usually September, when most rookies got their new instruments, so this was unusual for several reasons. As I would find out many years later, it was decided I should have some extra time to play *my* new instrument to better prepare me for beginner band in the fall. She was about the friendliest person I had ever met, and I had met a lot of friendly people. She even brought gifts.

We went to the basement where she gave me a folding music stand and pink-colored eight-by-ten music notebook called *Trombone Method for Beginners*. She showed me what all the moving parts were

actually for. The spray bottle wasn't a weapon but for keeping the slide lubricated so it would move easier. I think I liked it better before because as soon as I applied the oil, sprayed it, and went to move the slide, it shot across the room. Putting it back on was interesting. She showed me the seven *slide positions* and taught me my first note, *a B-Flat*. She showed me how to use the snake (I hated snakes but this was neat) to clean the insides of the horn and how to use the spit valve. *Spit valve*…how cool was that?

The absolute *coolest* thing was her. I don't know what she felt, but if she was nervous or bothered by my disability, she didn't show it. She didn't even seem to notice. She told me how everything worked, assuming I could, instead of deciding I couldn't. That was a huge distinction for me, and I think, for everyone.

The thirty minutes went by in a blur. When she left, she promised to see me every Tuesday after school. Right then, something inside me had changed. I raced back downstairs, opened my pink book, and started learning the notes. The slide mostly stayed on and the smile on Mom and Dad's face every time I came upstairs seemed bigger than usual. Something had definitely happened.

Maybe dreams don't always start when you are little. Maybe dreams begin the moment another person, or a story, or any number of points of inspiration collide with our life path. My life had collided with Blaine McClary and Cindy Knapp. Together, they changed my future. Maybe they were meant to be there, but I like to believe they made a choice.

I have an expression. Some of the most significant moments in our lives happen without us even knowing it. In hindsight, which is often with perfect vision, I can now say that. At the time, how could I know? What I did know was what these people were doing for me was astounding. That fact was never lost on me. What their reasons were, only they could say for sure, but I like to use it as another example of the immense power human beings possess to impact someone else, and the way we do that is not just about being positive. It's about understanding that unless people care more about others than they care about themselves, our reason for living will have less emptiness to fill.

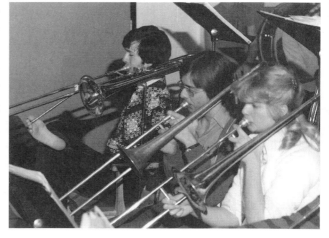

Mr. McClary chose to call Mom back after devising a scheme that must have sounded insane. He even dragged a couple of others along for the ride. Miss Knapp (who went on to become Mrs. Burham) chose to believe a little boy without arms could actually play a trombone rather than the much more logical choice she might have made. I guess I made the most important choice of all.

Sometimes you don't pick the dream; the dream picks you. How you respond can be everything.

chapter fifteen

wake up call

I was pretty happy to finish grade five, mostly to get away from Mr. Herauf. The summer meant yet another two months in paradise at Crystal Lake, except something was different. I had a new hobby and even though I didn't have to take my trombone and chair to the cabin (no room), I was instructed to take my mouthpiece and practice *buzzing* so my lips would stay in shape. I took it with me when I left the cabin, convincing Mom it was to rehearse, but in fact, it was mostly so I could do the fart noises and make my friends laugh. However, there was something else going on but I couldn't nail it down.

All summer long, Mom and Dad (when he came out) started to seem different to me. They hadn't bought a new wardrobe or changed their hair; they were just different. I found myself starting to argue with them and questioning some of the stuff I used to accept. They began saying stupid things, and to be honest, just seemed stupider. I guess I was becoming smarter, and especially since they barely finished elementary school. I was catching up. In fact, I was starting to prefer to not be around them.

All in all, it was a good summer, and September brought with it a few more changes. Not only was I going into grade six, we would now be the senior class in our school. This would be my last year at St. Al's. Junior high was next up and a lot further away, a lot further than across the street. I was also in the school band, which meant weekly practices at the junior high school. Band classes were held in the morning before school, but being in band was so cool it didn't matter. I probably didn't fully appreciate how much band would change my life because I was too preoccupied with something else.

I mentioned it before. Something was happening. My parents, my school, my routine, what was it? As if I didn't have enough to worry about, it seemed I was about to welcome new confusion into my life. Girls.

I'll tell you something in my usual seemingly insensitive matter. I fully agree with equality amongst people, but guys are guys and girls are girls and that's it. We are not the same, never have been, never will! Thank God. Well, thanks to a point. That difference caused me more confusion than almost anything else. I know, a bunch of guys out there just said, "Welcome to the club," and a similar verse chimed in from the gals. Seriously though, and this needs to be said, I had no idea what was going on.

It seemed to come with hints. Hints that had started in the middle of grade five. Other guys started making fun of me. It was subtle at first, but it was there. Even guys I thought were my friends were treating me differently. Or was I acting differently? See what I mean? Okay, everyone goes through puberty. We all suffer some kind of humility and confusion, but for me, it wasn't even something my buddies could relate to. In fact, it was their behavior that confused me the most. I wasn't getting picked for teams at recess or after school. I was getting excluded from the games we *all* used to play. To put it simply, I wasn't one of the guys anymore.

Sometimes they would surprise me, like the first time one kid showed me a Playboy magazine. I was impressed he would do that, but the pictures – most guys would go *wooah!* I was embarrassed. Plus, all my buddies seemed to be getting more muscular. Don't get me wrong, and sorry for the honesty, thalidomide only affected my arms, the other parts were just fine, thank you. It was like I wasn't as tough. Even though I was noticing the girls changing too, I wasn't sure what that meant. Keep in mind this was the early 1970s. Open discussions about heterosexuality versus homosexuality wasn't happening, especially not in Yorkton and *especially not at St. Al's.*

Listen, before you ask how I make this jump and for what purpose, I feel it's vital that this book be more than just a warm and fuzzy product. I hope people will be moved and motivated, but most important, myths will be exploded and self-examination will occur.

If society had been as open as today, my life would have been far less confusing. This seems to be a very contentious subject, yet it speaks to the stereotypes in our society. Guys are supposed to be masculine and women, feminine. When you start to debate those roles, you may as well be discussing politics or religion. I am not planning to explore this too far, but the roles I refer to became one of the most complicated questions in my development.

As the year went on, it was becoming harder and harder to fit in. My whole life was getting weird. I was spending more time at home alone, but I didn't want to be there because Mom was there. She was getting stranger by the hour. About the only thing going well was band and tap dancing, but you might imagine what the latter did to make things even cloudier. However, it seemed the biggest impact was AMPO.

Every year in May, all grade six students would go to outdoor education camp. We called it AMPO, which stood for the names of the three Yorkton Catholic elementary schools: St. Al's, St. Mary's, and St. Paul's, and then "O" for outdoors. Although the school board and all others concerned saw it as a practical educational and spiritual outing, we kids knew what really happened there. It was like a right of passage. AMPO carried with it all kinds of historic folklore, especially the naughty kind. It seemed that who you were, where you fit, and how the next few years of school would go were pretty much defined in one week at camp. As you might anticipate, I was in big trouble!

AMPO took place at a church camp at Good Spirit Lake (kind of appropriate name, huh?) and the setting was lovely. I was a lake veteran, but this was my first-ever camp experience. In the months and weeks leading up to camp, we were prepped for the experience in class. It seemed like I'd be able to participate okay. The camp was co-ed, but the sleeping accommodations, clearly not. That alone was adding stress, as the guy thing was getting worse. I wanted to stay with the guys, even though I was a bit afraid of what might happen, but I still needed help with the bathroom and dressing, my parents' domain.

I hoped Dad could come because I could still do the guy thing. But he had to work so guess who ended up making the trip? Mom was officially labeled *Parent Chaperone* but everyone knew, especially me, it was more like *Alvin's Mommy*. Don't get me wrong. I was used to

Mom traveling to various places with me because I needed help. But camp is supposed to be about your mom *not* being there and especially then. Even worse, while everyone else had their dorms, it was decided it would be most convenient for me to stay in a private cabin off the property with Mom. Imagine the effect.

I had never been embarrassed with my mom helping me before, but at AMPO, I noticed it for the first time. Many of the other kids were actually pretty good about it, especially the ones that didn't really know me. But yet again, the guys I thought liked me were inciting the other guys. I was bugged a lot. I suppose the one thing that kept me going was the girls weren't making fun of me. In fact, they were becoming such a distraction that I pretty much ignored the idiots. The girls would end up being the group I both adored and deeply feared but who would get me through the week. Girls! Actually, one girl in particular.

On the first night at camp we had a sock hop in the big hall. Thankfully, there was *our* music. I'm not sure about everyone else, but this definitely was my first sock hop. It was a blast because most dancing I could do. Remember, I was a tap dancer, but when the first waltz was played, things got real uncomfortable.

Good or bad, one of the sock hop rules on the first night was it was okay to dance with people you knew. But part of the plan was to make people dance with other people they didn't know – AMPO bonding, I guess. There were a couple of priests and some nuns there. This was also to be an exercise in *all children of God are beautiful* so nobody was allowed to be left out. In one of the more poignant moments of my life, the first waltz began. It was Donny Osmond's *Puppy Love.* Whatever matching system they applied, I ended up with a partner. And what a partner.

Her name was Charlene. Charlene was from another school. I don't remember which one. At that moment, I didn't even remember my name. She was beautiful. She was taller than I was but not by much. She was beautiful (did I mention that?). Waltzing meant getting close to each other, of course. My lack of arms added another dimension. Aside from my inability to lead, one had to wonder how I would do this. Once again, my history with Mom came into play.

We lived in Yorkton and that meant lots of dances. They were mostly wedding parties that seemed to happen all the time. Typical of smaller towns, we knew lots of people. If you grew up in a situation where this was not the norm, I'm sorry to brag about it. It was another piece of this puzzle of my life that was so positive. I learned to dance early, and Mom was always a willing partner. Most of these dances did not have rock and roll. They had polkas. They had a lot of polkas. They also had waltzes, which just seemed like slow polkas, but they all involved grabbing your partner and docey-doeing your feet off. Mom insisted I be grabbed. She would put her hands where they typically would go, one on the shoulder the other on my upper hip. Somehow, she would lead me but make me feel like I was doing the leading. The point is, I danced, and I had waltzed, even though it was with my mom. What I hadn't done was waltz with Mom to Donny Osmond's *Puppy Love*.

Since we weren't allowed to dance close, it made the closeness less close. I suppose Charlene was just a step above most people because she didn't appear at all uncomfortable. She told me her name. I told her mine. She just put her hands on my shoulders, and we started to dance. It was wonderful. That doesn't mean I wasn't nervous. I suppose Charlene was too, although she smiled the whole time. I smiled for a week. When the song was over, so was the dance. She said thanks and walked back to her friends. I don't remember them laughing or anything, but I've always wanted to know what they talked about.

The rest of camp went okay, but after a week, it was back to school. As much as I was still basking in the glow of *Puppy Love*, it seemed I had also been labeled. Let's face it; I was becoming one of the outcasts. I think my parents sensed that. I believe that altered their normal behavior, so instead of pushing my independence, they began a trend towards the opposite. I remember one incident in particular. Probably not a surprise, it happened after camp.

Boys being boys, in grade six, there was a game called *murder soccer*. Quite simply, it was full contact soccer where things normally penalized, like tripping, were totally encouraged. As seemed to be the trend, I was usually excluded from such games, but this time, I wasn't.

Who knows what was really going on? I viewed it as a test, not some biblical conversion on the part of all the guys who were now the bullies in my life. I was at first excited but very quickly felt intimidated. This particular game took place during the lunch hour. Since I went home across the street for lunch, I was always done quickly and back at school. Strangely, my dad had come home for lunch that day, which he had only recently started doing regularly.

So there we were, using a soccer ball to disguise a bunch of boys trying to knock the crap out of each other. I should have known better, but I was so hungry for acceptance. I was not tough. My only asset of physical ability: my legs and feet were my only tool of aggressiveness. They were not as important at that moment as my need for being a guy. I chased the ball, but my target was Bob Putz (not really his name). I wasn't after Bob in particular, although he was not one of my favorite people. I'm sure he didn't like me. Oddly, Bob and his family lived right across the street. We had played together as children, but for whatever reason, we had become adversaries. As I zeroed in on him, I kicked at his legs and tripped him. He went down like a rock. I grabbed the ball, but didn't get very far, as Bob got up and tripped me. But before he took the ball, he stomped on my ankle. The pain seared as hot as a branding iron. I screamed with agony. Nobody cared or at least they didn't show it. That was part of the game. I wish I wouldn't have screamed, but it really hurt. I should have gotten up, but I couldn't. What happened next was remarkable.

My dad had just come out to get in his old car to go back to work. The timing couldn't have been more bizarre. Dad raced across the street, ran over to me, shouted at the boys (Dad could shout), picked me up under my legs and back, and carried me home. I can still remember the trip home. I felt a warm comfort in my dad's arms but also felt a stark coldness looking back at the schoolyard and the guys who I wanted to be one of, almost knowing that something irreversible had taken place in my life. Meanwhile, I was in such pain.

When I got home, my parents reacted in a predictable way. They loved me so much my pain was their pain. Dad stayed a while, but being so dedicated to his job, he had to get back to work. Having iced my ankle and comforted me as much as possible, he left. Mom was beside herself. She made sure I was okay and went across the street to talk to the principal. It would be a meeting that would change school life. It would also change, temporarily, mine.

Mom was gone for a short time. When she returned, she bundled me up and took me to the doctor. My ankle had swelled and still hurt a great deal. I was sent to the hospital for x-rays, which determined a bruise so deep, it had dented my anklebone but had not fractured or broken it. It was the worst injury I had ever experienced; yet in the realm of things, I was lucky. I had already understood the damage to my body was minor compared to the damage to my heart. It wasn't the muscle that beat in my chest but the feeling one gets when a love is lost. I had lost much that day.

I had to stay home a couple of days but luckily, and to this day, I have always healed fast. When I went back to school, I knew things were different. What I didn't know was the principal had instructed the students to steer clear of me. I can appreciate his situation, but confusion ruled my life. I was alone. I had parents whose judgment might be questioned but loved me desperately. I had teachers who cared about me but also cared about the rest of their students. And, I had my peers who must have saw me with both pity and resentment. What I never got was an apology from Bob. I honestly don't know if I deserved it, but I did get hurt.

When I hear of young teenagers ending their life because they felt so alienated, so ridiculed, so picked on and laughed at and made to feel so insignificant that they see no future, I can identify. It is a pain that controls you. It is a pain that made my ankle feel nothing by comparison. The saying that 'sticks and stones can break your bones but words can never hurt you' was obviously written by someone who had never been bullied. I'm over forty, and writing this, I could feel the hurt. Yet, I had to write this. You know that expression, 'Time heals all wounds'? It does. Although the wound does leave a scar, you don't realize that it will pass with time, if you let it. All you know is the pain is the pain you feel right then. I am one of the fortunate who somehow went on. This playground incident also played a huge role in the beginning of my questioning my masculinity.

When Charlene danced with me, it was a rare light in an ever-darkening tunnel that made me wonder who I really was. I can't say I ever wondered if I was gay, mostly because that wasn't something debated, like today. But I felt so lost. I wasn't tough. I wasn't cool. I was Mommy's boy, and even with the guys, Dad had to rescue me.

I knew I liked girls. I sure liked Charlene, but along with all the girls, I felt patronized. Maybe they weren't doing that, but that's what I felt. I was beginning what would be the most difficult phase of my life. I'm pretty sure it was common amongst most preteens, but my reason for declaring it is for the reader.

I'm doing this book as an extension of my professional life. I have dedicated my career to helping people understand that challenge is not much fun but is a part of life. Some people are given more challenge than is at all fair. Asking the question, "Who am I?" has no easy answer. If you can identify, keep reading because, although I am not privy to the answer, I hope to encourage all who read this to never give up. Giving up may seem the only solution, but trust me, it is only one of a million.

chapter sixteen

change is good

Finishing grade six was filled with so many emotions. St. Al's was my second home and like my first home, took me in as an act of compassion. It was a place that planted many seeds. The planters were some of the best teachers a student could ever wish for. Like a garden full of bloom, there were also weeds that spoiled some of the beauty. Especially near the end with my soccer (murder ball) injury and accompanied alienation. It caused some anxiety for me, but it also caused some excitement because grade seven is usually a big year. Traditionally, it is the year that one changes schools, or failing that, it is the year we all change when puberty creeps in. We begin to *grow up*. I'm sure it's a big deal for everybody, but to personalize this, it was huge for me.

Until grade six, school was right across the street. Everything was so secure. I could run home anytime so easily, especially to use the washroom, because I couldn't do that myself back then. I had taken that convenience for granted. Junior high was six blocks away. It may as well have been six light years away. Although we frequented several areas of Yorkton, most of my life was a couple of square blocks surrounding my home. But I had been to the junior high school before.

In grade six, band practices were held at Dr. Brass Junior High School. Twice a week at 7:30 in the morning, we were directed by Mrs. Burham. I left my chair and trombone at the school (one of the lucky ones who didn't have to cart my instrument back and forth with even a greater excuse about not practicing at home). That was grade six. Now, I was much older.

Dr. Brass was an interesting school. It included two buildings, one of them Yorkton's first high school. The Yorkton Collegiate Institute, or YCI, was a historic building built in the early 1900s. In 1972, it was mostly boarded up and slated for demolition. The newer part was about twenty years old and had been a public school for grades seven, eight, and nine for many years. I'm not trying to be an historian here, but there was something important that I didn't really understand about what was happening in the upper circle of educational gurus in Yorkton.

The city was growing and quickly. More growth meant more kids and old traditions meeting the new. I'm not sure what the norm is, but in Yorkton, there were the public and Catholic school systems. It wasn't ugly, but there was a clear division between the two systems. When I started school at St. Al's, the school went as high as grade eight. After that, everyone would head to high school. In fact, Yorkton was quite famous for its two Catholic high schools: St. Joseph's College for boys and Sacred Heart Academy for girls. Most students were local, but some would come from across Canada to live and attend the schools. It was the essence of a religious education and all the instructors were clergy. Many future priests and nuns would find their calling while in these buildings. However, the world was changing and enrollment had been declining. There was also pressure to move away from the segregated model. It didn't help that right across the street from these two schools was the brand new Yorkton Regional High School. The timing couldn't have been more weird. I was to be a big beneficiary.

The decision was for Sacred Heart to become the new mixed Catholic secondary school and St. Joseph's would be sold to the public system and become the new junior high. There would be a transition phase of one year, the year I went to Dr. Brass. I could have gone to Sacred Heart, following my Catholic classmates, but ironically, band included both systems, and the practices were at the public school. So for logistics, more than anything, I found myself not only in a relatively new school, but the kids I'd called my classmates for six years were all gone. I thought I'd be alone, but something strange happened.

Homerooms at Dr. Brass would be divided into classes of around twenty-five students. Rather than being divided alphabetically, the format included academic standing, and in my case, band kids. I wasn't alone at all the first day of school. I knew almost everyone because most of us were in band. I didn't know them as close as my past peers, but that actually excited me. And it scared me. I was pretty much scared, period. Whoever invented the term *comfort zones* knew what they were talking about. However, something happened on the first day of classes that would prove to be another one of those *life-changing* events.

After lunch, we had our first music class. Alongside my mates, I walked into a room and spotted a very large woman. I know much of my discussion involves not caring about the outside but you do need to know what I saw. She was tall for a woman and she had, as they say, big bones. She carried a lot of weight. That was what you focused on the first time you saw her. The only thing that would change that focus was when she opened her mouth. If she was large in body, she must have also had really big lungs. We were pubescent. We made noise. This woman made more.

After going from volume to silence, you could hear a pin drop; we were introduced to Mrs. McClary. She would be our designated music teacher. There are people you meet in life that take you a long time to figure out. Then you meet people like Mrs. McClary. She would be memorable. You just knew that. The first thing that was obvious was you didn't mess with her. She wasn't rude or mean; she just took control. The second thing you noticed was she loved music. If that was the case, she must have had her good side, right? Actually, and this isn't about her size, she had many sides as I would discover, one that blew me away.

Mrs. McClary asked me to stay for a second after the bell rang. When everyone else was gone, she told me she knew about me. I don't know why I hadn't clued in, but when she told me her husband was Mr. McClary, I must have lit up. She talked to me about how impressed she was with my story and how glad they were that I had agreed to play trombone. She seemed so different. She was even bigger up close. Her warmth was magnetic. When we were done a couple of minutes later, she told me how much she was looking forward to having me in her class and gave me a little hug. It was the first of what would be hundreds of hugs and a new chapter of my life. It was being written by music and two of its authors lived in the same house.

chapter seventeen

who let the dog out?

Who ever really knows where the meeting of one human being will take you? As you might imagine, writing a book using retrospect allows great editorial license. What I am personally fascinated with is trying to recall what I was yet to know. I had no idea what role Myrna McClary was going to play in my life, but before I continue, let me again go back.

When I was around eight years old, I was put into something – I remember to this day – I had serious doubts about. Dad decided that since other kids were getting involved in out-of-school activities, so should his son. Obviously, choices were limited and not because it was Yorkton. So, in his infinite wisdom, Dad enrolled me in tap dancing. Clearly, I was not living in a democracy. Nothing against tap dancing itself, but why me?

Actually, I loved dancing. The horror I first felt faded quickly. What was a little weird was that I was the only boy. Let's remember, this was 1968 and boys in fine arts dancing were not looked at the same as they would now. Needless to say, the guys at school were kept in the dark. But this was Yorkton. Sooner or later it wouldn't be a secret.

In 1969, for a town the size of Yorkton to have its own television station was quite remarkable. It was a Canadian Broadcasting Corporation (CBC) affiliate and had the call letters CKOS. We always tongue-in-cheek called it KAOS, but it was a big part of local life. Most of the shows were from the network. Shows like *Front Page Challenge, Take Thirty,* and *Wayne and Schuster* were popular and icons of Canadian entertainment. The Yorkton icon was *Profile.*

Profile was all CKOS. It was written, produced, shot, and transmitted from the studios right on Broadway (even Yorkton had a Broadway). Most important, it profiled (Profile…get it?) local talent. With due respect (because I love Yorkton), talent was often a bit of a stretch. Yet, to make it on the show was a pretty big deal. So one fateful day at tap lessons, we were informed that fame had called our names.

In less than a month, the girls and I would make our world television debut. For the briefest of moments, I was thrilled. Television!

The media was very different then. Color television was in its infancy and one channel was it for Yorkton. No remotes, no digital cable or satellites, and definitely no recording devices. That last part would prove to be good and bad. Today, as was the case then, I imagine one thing hasn't changed: the opportunity to be famous was thrilling. But a moment later, it hit me. I would be famous all over Yorkton, which meant all my parents' friends would see me and probably spoil me. Conversely, all of *my* friends would see me. I'm sure spoiling me would not be their first priority.

The following couple of weeks were a combination of excitement and fear. We were pretty good. In fact, Mrs. Haft was the best tap teacher in town. How we would do was not in question. Still, we had a couple of extra rehearsals just to be sure, and just like that, the day arrived. I left the house. Mom and Dad stayed home to watch. Dad probably got on the phone as soon as the back door closed to remind *everyone* to watch. I'm pretty sure they all had it on their calendars.

I had never been in a television station. I still remember a time in my life when my nephew, Scott (one year older than me), had convinced me that the shows one watched actually took place inside the actual television itself. When I asked how they fit, he said they shrunk everything with a special machine, and that it was magic. I was little. What did I know? Having earlier determined Scott was pulling my leg, this was a genuine thrill. To walk into the studio and see the actual *Profile* set, I couldn't believe my eyes. It was in color! We had a black and white television.

We met the host Roger McGlauchlin. We may as well have been meeting Ed Sullivan. The magic moment came before you knew it. I wish I could remember the actual experience. When Roger introduced us as the dancers from *The Haft School of Dance*, the music began and off we went. We were perfect (had to be or Mrs. Haft would have kicked our butts), and just like that it was over. I wish I could have slowed it down, but it went so fast. We were expected to be flawless and that meant serious concentration. When the music started and the little red light on one of the cameras went on, it became so real. We were on television! I…I was on television! This was so cool. I even forgot about the guys. The whole world was going to see me on TV. Well, Yorkton and district that is, which for me in 1969 was the whole world.

After our dance, we were a hit. Roger asked us our names and how long we'd been dancing, thanked us again, and that was that. The euphoria lasted all the way home and got even better when I went in the house. Dad was so proud. The phone calls came from my parents' friends. Everything was perfect. Everything except this was a Tuesday. Tomorrow was a school day. Egad!

You know, it wasn't as bad as it could have been. I guess the weight of the actual tap dancing was lightened by the culture of celebrity. I suppose it helped a bit that we weren't wearing weird outfits with sequins and stuff, rather it was leotards for the girls, pants and a shirt for me. Even my tap shoes looked okay, although real shiny. What I didn't know was one of the people watching *Profile* on the other side of town was Mrs. Myrna McClary. She saw it and filed it away in her memory bank. It would be profound.

Being in Mrs. McClary's 1972 music class was special. I guess if you didn't like music, you might feel different. I heard there were actually people that loved math class; not me. To each his own. I was starting to feel very different about myself. There had been music at St. Al's but not like this. Just after classes resumed following Christmas break in 1973, it was announced there would be a musical production in the spring. Auditions would be held in two weeks, and everyone

could audition. The show was *You're A Good Man Charlie Brown*.

Well, I'd seen musicals on television, Fred Astaire being one of Dad's favorites, and I'm sure the inspiration for his son being a tap dancer. I'd seen the *Peanuts* cartoons. A musical about *Peanuts*? Then things got very strange.

After the next music class the following day, Mrs. McClary approached me and wanted to chat alone. She was definitely a favorite teacher of mine, so any attention from her was a bonus. She got real quiet again and asked me to do her a favor. She wanted me to audition for the part of *Snoopy*. Try to picture my reaction. If you can, send me a note because I can't imagine the look on my face. I guess I said, "What?" I heard her. Even in quiet mode you could hear her. She didn't repeat herself; she never repeated herself. She explained that Snoopy's part had a scene to himself. It involved a song done solo and (ready for this) a dance.

The song was *Suppertime*. The dance was to be done while singing the solo. Mrs. McClary decided I fit the part but she couldn't just give it to me. I fit the part of a dancing dog…brilliant.

Actually, her logic was intriguing. Snoopy walked upright most of the time and his front paws were usually at his side. I walked upright most of the time and had no front paws. Snoopy was a one-of-a-kind character. Enough said. Snoopy's part required a singer. I could sing. Snoopy needed to dance. She had watched *Profile* all those years ago and saw me dance. So why couldn't I be Snoopy?

Before I knew it, I was auditioning for the role of Charlie Brown's beagle. In a moment I will cherish forever, I came to school the next day, and posted on the hallway wall just outside the gym, was the list of who received the parts. My name was there. Right beside *Snoopy* was Alvin Law. Unbelievable.

Being in *You're A Good Man Charlie Brown* was pure joy. Every rehearsal, every performance, every moment was a feeling I had never experienced. I had always gotten attention. I had never witnessed a standing ovation. I believe the confidence that awakened inside of me came through the spirit of a Charles Schultz's character, but it was Myrna McClary that made it all possible. I know this to be fact: being *Snoopy* showed me a side of my life I had suspected was there right from the first time I climbed on stage at the Legion Hall at age three and sang, "You Are My Sunshine." But being part of a cast, performing a show, and hearing that applause, it is indeed hard to describe.

Grade seven started out being a year of opposites – the excitement of a new school and the terror of a new school. There were so many emotions. And looking back, such growth. Because of my love for music, school also became different. Although I still had rough days living with my differences, I loved being there. I will never know whether our paths were meant to cross. As I mentioned before, who knew that the day we met would be the start of such a special relationship and one that I would value forever.

Myrna McClary

Thank you, Mrs. McClary for being who you were. I'm sure you are still the same, but thank you for our time together. There were countless private vocal lessons in your home. There were more musicals, one written, produced, and performed by our grade nine music class (It was called *Money Tree)*. There were Job's Daughters conventions (The International Order of Job's Daughters is an international charity service organization.), where I sang solo for hundreds of girls (Barry Manilow man, it worked). But all through it was the joy. There is a spiritual song called *Make a Joyful Noise*. I thank Mrs. McClary for both: the noise and the joy.

chapter eighteen

drummer boy

In another of my life's strange twists, I found myself once again changing schools. That alone isn't odd, but to fill in some background, grade seven was at Dr. Brass Junior High, about six blocks from home. However, in keeping with the educational changes in Yorkton, Dr. Brass would become an elementary school. The new public junior high school would become St. Joseph's Junior High. St. Joe's was, for decades, the Catholic boys high school called St. Joseph's College. Sacred Heart High, the girls' school, was across the street. It became the new, integrated, coed Catholic high school. Why am I providing for you such apparently meaningless detail?

The physical transition was one thing, since St. Joe's was much further away, at least a mile from home. My year at Dr. Brass had taught me to adapt to the distance, so it simply changed my schedule. The real change was something not so obvious.

In grade seven, I felt like I had left much of the stress of my final year at St. Al's behind. I had a fresh start with a new school and new classmates who, although would kid around, didn't pick on me. The new school was across the street from the new Catholic high school. In that school, the classmates I thought were gone from my life were back. Some of the kids who might have gone to Sacred Heart chose St. Joe's. Their presence was both annoying and worrisome.

I spent a whole year with little anxiety, especially with my love for music growing, and my experience as *Snoopy* giving me a huge boost of confidence at a most opportune time. Now, that would be tested. I secretly wished that my old enemies from St. Al's might have matured and moved on, but junior high is not a hotbed of maturity.

It goes without saying that puberty is tough for *everybody.* It is much tougher when you're different. Just one thought. What makes one different? My theory is we spend most of our lives searching for similarities, and the journey begins with puberty. I'm sure it's mostly biology at first, and all those changes add to the confusion, but hear me out.

Adults congregate to things they share in common with other adults. For many, it begins in college because there, it's almost a prerequisite to be contrary. Although every generation believes they invented radicalism, it is the most predictable thing there is. Again, the irony in junior high and high school is it's horrible to stick out. In college, it's cool. After college, we again start to search out commonalities. We find a job that we have not only studied but are hopefully interested in. There we find another commonality. We vote for a political party that we agree with, hang out with friends who have similar interests and beliefs, and you get the idea.

The irony of adolescence is we are least prepared for being different when we feel the most difference; and that difference is enhanced by equally maladjusted teens who take out their own anxiety on the easiest and most common target: the most different. I definitely fit the *most different* category. Some of the guys who best knew how to push my buttons were back in the same hallways. They offered lessons to the other *cool wannabees.*

My St. Joe's experience was sometimes brutal. For months, I was teased, picked on, and laughed at. I didn't like it much but my grade six *tattletale* role was still fresh in my mind, so I kept it to myself this time. I really didn't need Daddy to come and stick up for me again. So, like all those who have experienced this dark world, I faked my life and wished every night that the next day would be different. But it never was, and for a while, I wasn't sure I could go on. Yet again, fate intervened. One day, my family met a young man named Curt Little.

One of the warm memories of childhood was living across the back alley from the Hansons. They were a super family who socialized a lot. My folks saw them all the time. They had four girls, who for me, were built in babysitters. They were amazing people for many reasons. A fire gutted their house one night, and they stayed with us for a couple of days. Instead of losing their grip, it strengthened their resolve to move on. I bring this up because they attracted great people to their lives.

This was passed on to their daughters. Their second oldest daughter was one of my parents' favorites. Her name was Gay.

I don't remember when, but the Hansons moved to Winnipeg. That was tough. We missed them so much that we would go to see them for special holidays, Easter being one of my favorites. Considering how grade eight was going, at least emotionally, I was so excited to go to Winnipeg for Easter. Having dinner at Hansons usually meant lots of people and lots of fun. For Good Friday, there were over a dozen. One of them was the coolest guy I had ever seen. He was Gay's boyfriend. His name was Curt. Gay would never have dated anybody but the best. He was more than just cool; he paid attention to me and even hung out with me. He was a drummer. It was amazing. He got permission to take me over to his house the next day (he lived with his parents) so I could see him play his drums. Was this the greatest guy ever invented?

He had a beautiful set of drums. They were black, Ludwig brand with Ziljian cymbals (all good, trust me). He could sure play. When he was done, I blurted out, "Man, would I love a set of drums like that!" What Curt said next was both unbelievable and depressing at the same time. He told me he was selling part of the kit, maybe I was interested? Interested, yes. Money, no. The logistics here are important. Curt had a big set of drums. I mean *big*. He had double bass drums and eight others, along with ten cymbals and all the hardware. He had been in a heavy rock band that was more show than music and decided to join another band more suited for his new interests. He planned to just store the extras, but decided a new drummer could use a break and use his surplus.

I have to tell you sometimes I wonder why stuff happens. That's a pretty common thought when it comes to bad stuff, but do we wonder the same thing about the good stuff? I sure do, especially this time. With the two extremes filling my head, we went back to the Hanson's. I sat my folks down and did the best sell-job I could. It was astounding. They didn't even say no. They said they would chat and were sincere. This wasn't like the classic parental brush-off. They even took Curt aside and talked to him.

It was late Saturday afternoon, and in a trip that even to this day, I can't believe, we were headed back to Curt's. Me, Curt, Gay, Mr.

Hanson (Bill), and my parents checked out the drums. An hour later, my new hero and all around great guy had taken the biggest bath ever and sold me a small set of pro-quality drums for two hundred dollars. That day would become a marker in my life. A changing moment in time and a springboard to heights I could not have even fathomed.

I will never forget bringing those drums home and setting them up in place of my old *token* drums, which, by the way, were better than having nothing. Putting them aside was a bit sad. However, this wasn't about buying something new, or in this case, used. Ready for some philosophical observation?

When I got the newer set of drums, it wasn't about being *bought.* I believe this is a major human flaw, especially among parents. Our kids

are depressed. Their lives are unhappy, so to make them happy, we buy them happiness. This chapter of my life would prove to be profound in the extreme, but when it happened, I didn't know that. All I knew was the drums changed my life for the moment during a time when I really needed something positive. All the anxiety at school actually became bearable simply knowing that after school, I had my drums to play. I truly *loved* to play.

The key is, the anxiety at school became *bearable.* It didn't disappear. It was still there. Life is full of anxiety, and nobody is immune. Learning to cope with it…that's the key. I know this sounds sweet, but when people ask me how I have dealt with the often-complicated emotions of my life, the answers are often quite simple. Therein lies its own irony.

For me, it was drums. For you, it may be jogging, painting, or a puppy. Find something to balance all of life's pressures instead of dwelling on them. My life is not perfect. Here in my forties, anxiety still exists, but I still have my drums. No, they don't get banged on every day, but even in their silence, they are a loud reminder of a monumental change in my life at a time when I needed something…anything to help me celebrate instead of mourn my own life.

chapter nineteen

the journey to self-acceptance

One of the ultimate ironies of life, and I use the word *irony* a great deal, is how when we are experiencing growth as a human, we often don't recognize it. Getting the drums at Easter gave me a new *fun* thing in my life, while school continued to be a strain on my self-confidence. I suppose part of that strain was my father retiring from his job at Mickelson's. All those extra hours he had on his hands made him get on my case. That made him a tad annoying. When you look back, you can make the pieces fit the puzzle because you've done that puzzle so many times. In 1974, two very important things in my personal development occurred. I didn't realize their significance at the time or how far apart, yet close together they philosophically existed.

I was out having lunch with Dad. We didn't go out for dinner very often, but once a month we would go to A & W™. We called it *Burger Saturdays*. It was a treat and one that I anticipated for weeks. Without harsh judgment, it is interesting how today's fast food generation has changed what going out for dinner used to mean. With certain exceptions, fast food is exactly that…fast. When I was young, it was the experience. I feel fortunate I got to experience the typical drive-in, in our case, A & W™. It was located about a mile outside of Yorkton, and you could not eat inside. When we first started going, you had to pull into the parking stall diagonally. To get service, you'd turn on your headlights. The carhop would come out and take your order. When it was ready, she (it was usually a she) would bring it out and place the specially designed tray on the side window, (I was always amazed the tray didn't fall) which was rolled down half way. I'm not suggesting that this generation's version of fast food will not be as memorable for them, I just believe my, or our, version had a certain charm.

As civilization rushed ahead, even Yorkton changed. One day, they installed intercoms at the drive-in. Although you still got the window tray, you could press a button and order without having to use your headlights. It was pretty cool, actually, but you could never really understand what they were saying when repeating your order. But change is inevitable. The owners of the A & W™ decided to move into town and build a brand new drive-in. It was pretty nice. You could still eat in your car and order through a much better intercom. However, the new place had inside eating, too.

At first, it was a novelty and quite exciting, but for me something was different. I soon realized what it was. I was used to people staring at me, but I just never ate in public. Actually, I did, but it was usually perogies or a burger at the curling club, chips at the bowling alley, or a sandwich at the golf course. In those places, *everyone* knew me. We didn't go out any other time except *Burger Saturdays*. When we were in our car (in the early days, a 1957 Chevy…how cool is that?), I was comfortable. You see, eating a hamburger with your toes can often be, well…messy! I have to squish it between my big and second toe. When the burgers are loaded…okay, you get the picture. I even lick my toes off when I'm done, but you probably don't want to know that.

Along came our special day, but Mom couldn't come with us this time. Dad and I ordered a Papa Burger (double patties, onions, pickles, mayo, mustard, and ketchup, just in case you don't know) and a Root Beer in a big frosted mug. (Excuse me. I just have to run out to A & W™.) As I took my first bite, I spotted a stranger across the restaurant. He was hard to miss because the look on his face said it all. He was staring at me with that blank, rude expression that a book makes difficult to describe, but I'm sure you can imagine it. Let's be honest, I know why people look at me, especially when eating, but some respect would be nice. This guy looked like he was ready to puke. It was offensive, and I was offended. I guess I just had enough.

So when the guy stared at me, I felt a need to respond. I suppose I could have stared back and made an *I'm gonna puke* face. I could have put my burger down, gone over, and chatted with him, or better yet, kick him in the head. But I was sitting across from my dad, the ex-boxer who didn't believe in violence. I had to do something. I wished I had a rock…but I had a burger. He wasn't very far, and I had really strong legs. I was measuring the trajectory when Dad blurted out, "What are you doing?"

"Aiming," I answered.

"You're what?"

"Aiming. There's a guy staring at me!"

Calmly, Dad replied, "Alvin, you are eating a hamburger in a restaurant with your foot."

"Yeah, and I'm gonna throw it at him 'cause I'm being insulted!"

He giggled a bit and reminded me I couldn't do that. So I freaked. I yelled at him to do something. The yelling froze time. Dad didn't move. He just stared at me. He looked over his shoulder at the guy, looked back at me, and said, "You didn't like it, huh?"

I was really hoping he would get up, go over to the guy, and punch his lights out. Trust me, it would have been easy for Dad. One hit and it would have been over. But that wasn't his style. He leaned across the table and said, "Tough."

"What?"

"Tough, kid. Alvin, you may want to realize something. You are going to get stared at everyday for the rest of your life. If you don't like it, stay home. Or deal with it and move on." Thanks, Dad.

Why does reality seem to hurt more when you're in puberty? Why does the messenger become the enemy? I am curious about a lot of things but at the top of the list is why it's so common to idolize your parents as a child, hate them as a teenager, and use them as your inspiration when raising your own family. It is weird isn't it? I will never forget that day.

There is a story (one of those) that says the day a child stops being a child, an imaginary creature steals them, replaces them with a teenager, and if you're lucky, some day you'll get your child back as an adult. I've seen it happen in my house with my son Vance. It happened to Jack and Hilda Law. Like Vance, (I'm sure he thinks he got the worst part of the deal having me and Darlene for parents) I hated my parents. Almost impossible to imagine. These wonderful, unselfish, loving people who sacrificed so much for me became my mortal enemies.

I finished my burger, even though my appetite was gone. We went home in silence. I raced to my room, slammed the door, flopped on my bed, and sobbed. I had never felt so sad. I had to be the ugliest freak ever born. Why me? What did I do to deserve this? My life was the worst. It felt empty, like I had used all the gas I had in the tank to get me to that moment and there was nothing to take me any further. I got up, took off my shirt, and posed in front of my bedroom mirror. Guys do this. I don't know if girls pose. Guys flex and bulge and act like it's a bodybuilding contest. I looked at myself and felt pathetic.

How could I ever be a man? Men are strong. Men have muscles, big chests, strong, ripped abdomens, and big broad shoulders. Arms. Men have arms. This was not going well. Strangely, out of the corner of my eye, I spotted my artificial arms. Sitting in the corner of my room were my almost new, very high-tech, very expensive, imported myo-electric prosthetic appliances – imported from Germany, same as thalidomide, how ironic.

I lifted them on the bed, laid them on their back, lay on my back, and with my foot, closed them on my front. I pulled the Velcro straps tight, did up the Velcro buttons on the shirt. The shirt was already on the arms as I only wore it with the arms. Mom always removed and sewed up the sleeves of my everyday shirts. I stood up, again, I looked in the mirror. I looked different. I looked good. Except for the face and hair, I looked like a stud. Best of all, I looked like a man. Why do boys want to be men and men want to be boys? Why do some people believe that the path to true happiness begins on the outside? Good questions.

I started wearing the arms as much as I could. My parents were confused. They didn't believe I needed them, but had no choice due the doctor's edict. They really didn't know how I felt. Maybe the prosthesis was for the best. Maybe the theory of using my feet and dealing with the world was asking too much.

I didn't wear them to band, for doing chores, or even to school regularly. I did wear them at home a lot and dedicated myself to working with them to get more fluid and more natural. Even though a little voice told me I was being silly, I liked having a new image reflect back when I looked in a mirror. It was practically a stranger, but what had become familiar, I had grown to hate.

I knew things had changed when I was informed I had to make yet another trip to Toronto for therapy. For the first time in my life, I got excited about a trip to the hospital. Maybe my therapist could help me get better with the arms, and I could kiss the freak goodbye. Everyone noticed my improved cooperation. We were also trying something new.

It seemed that my frustration of people's reaction to my table manners was not such a surprise. It was, in fact, one of the focal points of the whole movement of the government assisting the thalidomiders by providing prosthetics rather than *real* help. When society saw us using artificial limbs, it made *them* feel better. I suppose that would be enough for us to play along. My therapist started taking me out of the hospital. The idea was simple; help Alvin blend in.

We went to stores, to museums, to the Science Center for its *hands-on* exhibits. Things were going so well, one day I got a special treat. We were going to a football game. Not just any game, but a game with the Toronto Argonauts of the Canadian Football League. It wasn't the Saskatchewan Roughriders, but it was CFL football, and I got very excited.

On her day off, my therapist came to the hospital and picked me up. Wearing the arms, of course, away we went. I think it was Exhibition Stadium, although not certain, but I clearly remember it was big. Big with lots of people. Big with lots of strangers. I didn't like strangers. That many of them made me nervous, but anything to exorcise the freak with the fake arms. We were about halfway up in the stands, near the twenty-yard line. It was a warm day. I was uncomfortably squeezed into the tight bleachers. The game was okay. As the second quarter began, I became very thirsty. I was trying to avoid using the arms because as real as they looked, they still made noise. They were electric.

My therapist must have been thirsty too. When she ordered two soft drinks, she passed one to me. I was on the spot. I had to grab the drink with my hand. So with my little shoulder bone, I reached forward to push the first button inside my shoulder compartment, the up button. The plastic and metal arms jerked into motion, a barely audible whine emanated from the elbow motor. It wasn't very fast, so it probably took ten seconds to reach the drink, while people around me were acting like there was a fly or mosquito buzzing around. I grabbed the drink by pushing the second button to open the cosmetic hand, the third to close it, and back to the first to complete the required action. The drink slowly approached my face. The strangers around me were still minorly distracted by the noise. As it reached about six inches from my face, it stopped. The arm stopped – right in front of my face, just far enough that I couldn't even bend my neck forward enough to reach the straw. Unbelievable!

Pretend you're me. You are in the middle of an adolescent identity crisis. You hate your parents. You hate your home. You hate your town. You hate everyone at school. You hate yourself. You hate being handicapped, people staring, people laughing, being picked on, called names, being made fun of, and avoided. You are ugly, scrawny, weak, and generally appalling to all who see you. You can't even go out to lunch without causing a mass wave of nausea. You're trying to hide, trying to fit, trying to *blend*, and your arm stalls. Right in front of your face, it just goes dead. I stared at it, and a voice inside me screamed, "C'mon baby!" The drink just sat there, hovering in mid air.

I had to do something. I couldn't be noticed. I couldn't fail. These were electric, right? What if I pushed all the buttons, all four of them at the same time? Maybe that would send a power surge to the motor and that would make it move. So I did. I held all four buttons. Ten, twenty, thirty seconds. Nothing. A minute. They didn't move a millimeter, but I heard a noise. It was the kind of noise you get when you touch the two free brass ends of automobile booster cables together after they're already hooked up to the car that's running (please don't go out and do this to find out what it's like…just trust me). They were loud, but not that loud. All of a sudden, I smelled smoke. Electrical smoke. I looked at my shoulder and faint, blue smoke came floating out of the collar of my shirt. Excellent. Now I was on fire too!

Actually, there was no fire, but there was a short, and the right arm was dead. No up, no down, no open the hand, no nothing. Clearly, this was one of those moments in time you immediately know you will never forget. You also know you have to do something. Being the emotional pinball that I was, I just lost it. Without any contemplation of the consequences, I removed my right shoe and sock, bent my leg up, and with my right foot, literally yanked the drink from the clutches of my right hand. I reached up further under the frozen hand and arm and had a drink. Please visualize this. The artificial hand that looks as real as yours is still parked right in front of my face, smoke is coming from the collar of my shirt, and I have a drink in my foot.

I can imagine the look on your face right now. Imagine the look on my therapist's face. The people around me were pretty focused now, all with the same look on their faces. That image is riveted in my mind. My therapist was not pleased. We left. What else could we do? I suppose we could have taken my arms off, let me use my feet, and enjoyed the rest of the game. But we didn't. We went back to the hospital and back to my room. She ripped off my arms (you know what I mean) and left, promising to be right back.

When she came back a short time later, she had mellowed. She came over to my bed, sat down beside me, and started to cry. She wasn't sobbing, just that cry you have when you can't think of anything else to do. I was fourteen. I didn't know what to do, so I apologized for wrecking the arm. She told me to forget it and said it was she that was sorry. I truly don't remember her name. Isn't that weird? I spent a lot of time with her and went through a lot, but I can't remember her name. I do remember what she said.

"Alvin, I'm going to recommend you no longer have to wear your arms. It's not because you wrecked them. In fact, when I saw you reach up with your foot, under the arm and hand, I saw how silly this all has been. Alvin, I went to university. I attend training programs on the latest technology and techniques. I try to be the best therapist I can, but today you made me realize something I hadn't thought of before. Not everyone needs fixing. Especially when they were never broken in the first place. How could I make you any better than God already did."

Wow.

I never saw my artificial arms again. I found out they were taken apart and given to two other amputees who really needed them. I didn't go through a *born again* conversion that day. In fact, the only noticeable change was with the arms gone, there was no confusion about what I had to do. My happiness would have to start with self-acceptance. In time, it might even transform into unconditional love. That day in Toronto would be the beginning of a journey that, realistically, I continue to travel to this day. It will probably never end. But it had a start, and that is better than never giving up.

Just imagine it.

is for never give up

Never give up! Easy to say, hard to do.
The biggest enemy we will ever have we
encounter every time we look in a mirror.
Yet mirrors do not reflect who
we truly are — our lives do.

chapter twenty

breakthrough

I feel compelled to fill you in on something I suspect you might be asking. This isn't a very big book. It's almost done, but we are only in as far as grade nine. You guessed right; there's another book. My reasoning is quite simple. This book shadows my speech. Trust me. I've thought about this a great deal, both this book and the speech. Obviously, much has happened in my adult life, but I feel strongly that my success in life was rooted in my youth. Although it's tempting to see this as a book for youth, I think it has a universal appeal when applying the Laws to every life: young, middle-aged, or old. This chapter will begin tying all my struggles to the inevitable because when I have my own reflections, it's tough to just skip a segment for brevity. What happened after my finally ridding myself of the artificial arms was monumental, so hang in there because the momentum is about to pick up big time.

I finally found out why I kept getting arms, over and over again. With respect, the doctors had badgered my parents about prosthetics. Even the evidence of not needing them didn't change their tune. They simply couldn't see the forest for the trees. In fact, when I was much younger – and I have a letter to prove it – they actually threatened my folks. If I didn't start using my arms as prescribed, which was pretty much always, they would remove me from their foster home and place me with more cooperative people. Bizarre, huh?

I mention this because my therapist recommending my prosthetic therapy be discontinued was huge. The weight, metaphorically and literally, had been lifted off my scrawny shoulders, but the relief for my parents must have been indescribable. There was only one flaw in the new plan.

I had huge buckteeth. That made the Alvin-and-the-Chipmunks abuse from the not-so-nice kids even worse. So, with freed up government cash, Mom set forth to get me braces for my teeth. Again, very common for my age, but for many kids, the worst hardware they could ever dream of. Strangely, my new view of the world made getting braces somehow okay. They were very uncomfortable, especially when playing trombone (I used wax). I really didn't complain because this was a physical improvement I could agree with.

Honestly, I was starting to understand myself. The saga of the burger and being stared at, my Dad saying get over it, and the ridding myself of the fake arms actually opened my eyes to something: my own forest and trees. I was okay. In fact, I was lucky. I was in band, choir, had returned to regularly attending my parents' church (in that choir too), and I now had pretty special, real-life friends. No surprise they were *music geeks* too. I had found my place. Even with short toes, I was a musician, and I wasn't alone.

I had new drums at home and was even receiving snare drum lessons. I was in grade nine, which also made me a school senior. I was promoted to lead chair trombone in the intermediate band. It was weird. Even my marks improved. The year flew by.

The following spring, I received a great surprise. The band department suggested to my parents that I go to summer jazz camp. You didn't have to try out, but you had to be pretty decent to cut it, so this was good news. True, Mom still had to come to camp, but this time I stayed in the dorm with the rest of the jazz freaks.

I need to say this. I honestly can't believe how much my mom sacrificed for me. In this case, she discussed my situation with the camp directors. They generously provided a free, private room for Mom and covered her meals as well. She kept out of my way, but amazingly, was always there if I needed her (bathroom and clothes again).

Another great thing happened in the spring. Our music class (with Mrs. McClary still at the helm) wrote, produced, and performed a musical. It was called *Money Tree* and was very loosely based on the Bromfman family and the prohibition history in Saskatchewan. We were also graduates that year. At the ceremony, I shared *Music Student of the Year* honors with my best friend, Stew Smith. I had a new best friend; life was truly getting better.

Jazz camp was incredible for a million reasons, but my favorite two I need to tell you about. The instructors at camp were truly world-renowned. Little did I know the camp, located in the Qu'Apelle valley in Saskatchewan and called Fort San, had a very respectable reputation and attracted some of the best in professional jazz. They were *very* cool but also very tough. Best of all, they didn't feel sorry for me. I was there to learn, play,

Summer Jazz Band Clinic, 1975, Fort Qu'Appelle

and improve. I was used to hard work. This was a whole new level. As a result, I left camp totally committed to music, especially jazz.

I also left camp with a new skill. Jack Mouse, the awesome leader of the percussion department, surprised me one day. I was jamming after class with a few other campers. We started trading instruments just for fun. It sounded bad, but it was so much fun. I convinced them to let me play drums. I was passionate. I had become quite efficient at the snare drum, but the obvious problem was, I was playing an instrument designed for four limbs with two.

Mr. Mouse strolled in. He laughed at us then gawked at me. It was, however, a great gawk. After we finished being creative, Jack (he insisted I call him that) asked me to stay. He was so kind, gentle, and groovy (still the 1970s). He sat behind the set and showed me something I'd never considered. I need to get a bit technical here, but drummers use one foot to play the bass or kick drum to lay down the foundation of the beat and the other to snap the high-hats, the horizontal pair of smaller cymbals connected to each other and a pedal to move them up and down. Clearly, using the sticks between my toes and playing the top drums and cymbals, I couldn't use the theoretical, most important elements of particularly, the jazz drummer.

He started playing without using his feet and just played. He then gave me the tip of my drumming life. Don't worry about the hi-hats. For the kick-drum, use my left foot and stick to hit the floor-tom (the big drum that sits next to the snare). It was brilliant. After he showed me, he got up and told me to let it rip. I did. I wasn't great, but his smile was as bright as any I've seen. I already had a drum set, but now, I could actually play it. This would be another pivotal moment in my life. I'm not exaggerating.

My jazz camp experience was, for me, better than ten trips to Disneyland. You couldn't wipe the chrome smile off my face (braces, remember?) for weeks. I returned a much-improved trombonist, and I now had a passion for playing the drums that made me feel a joy I had never experienced.

To make things even better, I was now in high school, and I wasn't even scared. I was pumped. I still had some insecurities but it felt like the dark days were finally in the shadows. Then, something even more spectacular happened.

Yorkton was becoming known for its music program. The senior level was based at the Yorkton Regional High School. One of the most

Alvin front row, middle

revered groups was called *The Troubadors*. They were known in the era as a *swing choir* (today regarded as a jazz chorus). They did some jazz but mostly pop. They had matching outfits made of very cool polyester (the era again). They had a four-piece rhythm section, did choreography on a full stage, and sang in four-part harmony. They were the best around. Making the choir was not easy.

Mrs. McClary encouraged me to audition. I pretty much humored her because, in my mind, my chances were miniscule. It wasn't that I couldn't sing well enough. I was missing what I perceived as a compelling component; they were very cool. I was not. But I had also begun adopting another approach to life. What did I have to lose?

I sang my best. I wasn't even nervous about my chances being so remote. It was a Friday. Monday they would post the results. I didn't even go look at the posting of the group. It was Stew Smith who broke the news. We'd made it! Both of us! *Unbelievable!*

Do you notice a pattern forming here? I did. It hit me like a brick. So I didn't have arms. So what? I had discovered my gift – well others had discovered it, but you already read that. I was not handicapped. I had a talent. The more I worked it the better the results. Okay, it was an obvious revelation but no matter how one discovers it, the empowerment is enormous.

Grade ten would be a blur of school, music, and growth. It wasn't perfect. I was still living in the subculture. I wasn't one of the populars. I wasn't cruising the halls with the girls going *ooh-baby*, and I still had a serious curfew at home. But I was practicing everything I could play or

sing, and I must say, I was happy. That was until I got the news that kind of threw a wrench in my new enlightenment. I was going to Camp Easter Seal.

chapter twenty-one
camp easter seal

I'd heard about Camp Easter Seal. I was actually surprised I hadn't been before and more surprised that I went to Fort San for Jazz Camp first. But, it made sense when I got the news. I'd been set up. Sure, I could go to Jazz Camp again, but only if I went to Camp Easter Seal, too. Look, there was no way I was going to Gimp Camp. Sorry if that appears rude, but I wasn't happy. Getting rid of those arms meant closing out the book on being a gimp. Now I had to go to a place that focused on exactly that. It was a wheelchair-blind-deaf-mute-shaky-spastic, and generally messed-up person place (was I sixteen or what?). Why did I have to go?

Somebody, probably a nosy, do-gooder motivational speaker type, convinced my parents I needed to go somewhere without my mom in tow to not only encourage my independence but give her a break from caring for me. I agreed with getting away from Mom, and even Dad for that matter, but why Gimp Camp? I wasn't a gimp, and there would be so many of *them* there. Ooooooohhhh, yuck! The drool, the diapers (they all wear diapers, don't they?), the screaming. Maybe I'd catch something and my legs would fall off! No. There was no way I was going to Gimp Camp. That's what I thought.

Except, you see, my theories about security, independence, and tough love (I never went to a seminar) began with Mom and Dad. Although they had the occasional glitch, they generally practiced what they preached. So, whether I liked it or not, we loaded up the orange Hornet (that's what it was; Dad loved AMC), drove the three hours to Watrous, the closest town, and then down to Manitou. With due respect, it was kind of smelly. In the middle of landlocked Saskatchewan is a salt lake. Since I was sixteen and melodramatic, I took it as a sign of biblical proportions. What was that place? The Sea of the Dead? The salt and its resulting organic byproducts created a smell that added so much to the now real nightmare unraveling before my eyes. It really was Gimp Camp. They were everywhere!

I was at my best worst humanly possible. I was whiny. I was hostile. I had the *death stare* down pat and was using it. Every step got worse. Cabins with ten little single foam-mattress beds, public toilets, and showers. Remember, Mom was still helping me dress and go to the toilet, including the wiping thing. I wanted to be away from them, but who would wipe my…oh my God!

I pretty much lost my composure. I even started to cry – for real, but of course, this was becoming a "Boy That Cried Wolf" saga. I had screwed myself. With the ultimate in stiff upper lip, my parents kissed me goodbye, headed to the orange Hornet and left. They left! Wow!

This was uncharted territory for me. This was my own Lewis and Clark, Christopher Columbus, Jacques Cousteau adventure. Okay, maybe not so big a challenge, but it felt like I was entering into a chamber of horrors, a true nightmare. No matter how much I wished it, I would not wake up. I thought my parents loved me. How could they do this? I needed to find a lawyer; oops, wrong generation. I didn't even pretend to handle this. I was miserable and wanted everyone to know it. In another of life's ironies, as much as my parents were living angels, they had not made me face my reality as well as they could have. Granted, a huge part of this was logistics. There just weren't clothes I could put on by myself. There wasn't any device that could tend to my toileting. That seems so funny to me now, but that day, I didn't laugh, not once…*and no one was going to make me!*

Actually, I suspected for years and was eventually told that my parents suffered more that day than I did. I wonder if by seeing all the other kids there, they started to question their own beliefs. They were told by scores of people, especially doctors, that their expectations of me were a little beyond reality. Sure, I had done some amazing things: the trombone, drums, driving a boat, even making it through regular school to almost grade eleven. But, I couldn't dress myself, do the bathroom and so many other elementary tasks. That was probably one of the worst days of all our lives.

To be poetic, with every new day comes a new light to guide the way to the undiscovered. I had been to many hospitals and many a nurse and orderly had seen my *full moon*. Since there were similar professionals at camp, I buried my pride, yet again, and cooperated enough just to cover the basics. I slept lousy, as if that would prove a point, went to breakfast, and didn't eat, another point, and went off to orientation. We stayed in cabins of ten, although there were only nine in mine. We were divided into activity groups so we could *bond* with other gimps. It took most of the morning for our activity group to see the sights. The nature of most of the campers meant slow would be the operative expression. That further frustrated me because I was mobile. Let's move it! How depressing.

Then came lunch. Great. Mass produced gimp slop. This couldn't be happening. My life was over. What life? Right. Good point. I had no life. I had almost no friends. I wasn't popular. I wasn't a star of one of the school teams. I didn't exactly stroll the hallways of the old YRHS and have the girls all going, ooooh baby! I was sinking fast. I had to escape. I had to bust out. Maybe I could scale the wall – guess not. As if things couldn't have been more dreadful, they appeared at the front of the Slop Hall. Two counselors: hippies it seemed, with acoustic guitars and smiley happy faces. Then it happened – Kumbaya. Aaarrgghh!

They sang it and made us sing it. Let's be real honest here. Most gimps can't sing (my sixteen-year-old opinion), and they were encouraging them. I had to get out. Then, as if the Lord Himself cranked up his million-watt spotlight, a divine image appeared in the doorway. It was real. It was Kelvin!

If you recall from earlier chapters, I had a roommate in my first memorable hospital stay in Regina. He was from the Swift Current area of Saskatchewan and was born without legs. I knew him quite well, and now he was here. He must have been sent to rescue me. Maybe he had a van out front we could tunnel under the wall. I could tunnel and Kelvin could crawl. We were different but the same. In fact, like me, Kelvin kept getting fake parts, too, which is why we kept running into each other, clinically speaking. When not forced to use the clunky prosthetics, I used my feet and legs for hands and arms; Kelvin used his hands and arms for feet and legs. Is that weird or what? This time, he was in a wheelchair. He also looked grumpy. What was he really doing here?

Could it be? Was it possible? Did Kelvin have the same kind of parents I had? Mean, uncaring, ruthless, selfish (insert every possible negative term ever invented here), hateful people? Maybe they'd gone to Vegas together, all four of them, drinking, gambling, staying up all night, not a care in the world because their loser kids were at Gimp Camp. Possible.

He spotted me right away. With a flattering gesture, he smiled. He wheeled over and pulled in beside me. It seemed Kelvin was glad to see me. I know I was glad to see him. He had a way about him that I admired. He also scared me a bit. Kelvin was very charming. He used that to explore the limits of his world. It also got him into mischief, which occasionally led to getting in trouble. I have often been described by those who knew me then as having quite the attitude, but that rarely extended to mischief. I just didn't like trouble. I was the annoying goody two-shoes kid who always went "Shhhh," the moment the teacher left the room. So kids like Kelvin were appealing but scary. Kelvin could be trouble. I was so glad to see him.

Unlike me, Kelvin was a Gimp Camp veteran. He also shared my feelings about being there. Oh sure, he explained, it was okay when you're a little fart, but there was absolutely nothing cool about being here now. Those were my feelings exactly. However, there was one indisputable fact. This was Monday and camp wasn't over until Saturday. We had to figure out a way to get through it. Just like the hospitals, we would do it together.

The first thing he did was critique the *Kumbayaers*, calling them lame, pardon the pun. Then he said, "Let's get out of here." Although my first impulse was to stay and be safe, I needed to get out more. He took me on the unofficial tour, enlightening me about past adventures and places to go when you just needed some space. We ended up at our cabin – *our cabin*. Kelvin was the tenth camper. This was getting better by the minute. I mourned his bed being on the opposite side of the cabin, so we did a switch. We moved the beds, lockers, everything.

I, of course, just had to say, "Won't we get in trouble?" to which Kelvin informed me that our cabin supervisor and him were tight.

So began a change in my feelings about being stuck there, and as it turned out, a change in my character. Aside from showing me his secret spots, Kelvin also coached me on how to deal with camp. It was actually quite fascinating. Kelvin may have been mischievous, but he was a good person. He wasn't mean. He used his charm in all kinds of ways. It seemed simple, actually, but it took some practice. Participate in activities, even if they seem stupid. Help those who need help, and most important, get on the good side of the counselors. Ironically, that seems to be a good recipe for life.

What was really weird was I was starting to have fun. There became a string of firsts. I rode a horse, shot a pellet gun, played volleyball (which was designed for the immobile but also worked for me), and countless other activities all designed for handicapped access. My favorite was archery. The bow was not like competition bows; it was probably from K-Mart, but it worked for me. Whenever I could, I'd be at the range shooting at targets. I even got to go there alone, a real perk given as a treat for good behavior. I was following Kelvin's lead, trying to be decent. The more I did that, not only did I have more fun, the days flew by. The nights became the most fun.

Kelvin and I were amongst the oldest kids there. If I remember right, the camp was for twelve to sixteen year olds. Part of the logic, I guess, was for the older ones to show the younger ones some of the tricks to making life a little easier. There were lots of staff to make sure we were healthy and safe, but independence was encouraged. The older you were the more rope you were given. There was a curfew, but as long as you used your brain and kept your nose relatively clean, the counselors tended to look the other way. So after the nightly campfires and sing-a-longs (yes, I even got into those too), us older kids would hang out. We couldn't stay out too late. We still had to go back to our bunks. Morning came early, but it was so much fun. I sensed there was something else happening. What seemed to bother me most at the beginning was now very compelling. I saw all these *gimps* but did not include myself as one of them. But I was one of them. There seemed to be some knowledge here that had been eluding me.

I always knew having no arms made me different. Because of how special my parents were, their friends, and Yorkton, I was made to feel special. But like every teenager out there (some more, some less), you reach a point where being different isn't cool. Whether people want to admit it or not, we all need acceptance (some more, some less). Because of all the complications of puberty, that need seemed magnified. Ironically, I found myself in the middle of a group of people who had a lot in common. It created our bond and felt so good. Here, I was not alone. Nobody likes to be alone. Little did I know that my anonymity was about to end and my first fifteen minutes of fame about to begin, as Pop Art icon Andy Warhol would have said.

On the Thursday, a television crew from CFQC-TV, a Saskatoon television station, came to camp to do a feature story. Camp Easter Seal at Lake Manitou had a long history and was well known. It was run by the Saskatchewan Council for Crippled Children and Adults,

Fishing at Camp Easter Seal

the SCCC&A (now known as the Abilities Council, a much better name), which operated it completely through donations. It had a very high profile, so the press was quite a common sight. Either by chance or by divine intervention, as the camera crew scoured the camp searching for inspiring imagery, I happened to be at the archery range. Let's be honest, the sight of me using my feet for almost anything gets attention. Some things I do received more attention than the others. The reporter did a beeline right to me and asked permission to film me and do an interview. Cool.

That night, I was on Saskatoon television, and the next day, all across Saskatchewan. That Friday afternoon, I met Gord Tanner. He had come from Saskatoon looking for me. He explained he was the Community Relations and Fundraising Director for the SCCC&A and one of his responsibilities was conducting the Easter Seals campaign for Saskatchewan. I had a strange premonition. He went on to tell me he saw the television feature and was very impressed. They had received a lot of calls praising the story and the camp, even some unsolicited donations. He wondered if I might consider being the Easter Seals *Timmy* for 1977. I couldn't believe my ears.

My mind raced back to Lake Simcoe and Whipper Billy Watson. My earliest dream of what I wanted to be someday. (I'll tell you this story in the next chapter.) That day had arrived, and I wasn't expecting it at all. I'm sure I blushed, because even today, more than twenty-five years later, I still remember the warmth that flooded my body. Mr. Tanner helped. He was tall and imposing, gray, almost white hair, and a smile that reminded me of Santa Clause. He must have been Santa Clause, but this was August.

I guess I said yes, but I'd have to ask my parents. He smiled again and said he already talked to them in Yorkton. If I wanted to, it was okay with them. I guess they weren't in Vegas after all. Wow! What a genuine thrill. I realize we have come a long way since *Timmy* and *Tammy, ambassadors,* and *poster children* were acceptable. There are many who think it's exploitive and patronizing. They are entitled to their opinion. I think they should mind their own business. I was right and truly honored to be asked to represent Easter Seals and all of the handicapped children who would benefit from things like Camp Easter Seal (Mr. Tanner told me calling it Gimp Camp might not be a good idea).

The next day was the last day of camp, so Kelvin and I decided a celebration was in order. Unfortunately, I couldn't tell him about my news. I was sworn to secrecy, as were my parents. I couldn't tell anyone until the New Year. Ah, the price of fame. Anyway, what we decided, as a radical way of finishing Camp 1976, was to convince our cabin supervisor to let us sleep outside that night: Kelvin and me, a couple of sleeping bags, and the Saskatchewan sky.

There was, naturally, an ulterior motive. We could stay up as late as we wanted. That night was special. Another oath of secrecy prevents me from revealing specifics, but there could not have been a better way to finish off my first and last camping experience at Lake Manitou.

Even that night, I knew I had changed. I believe strongly what changed me was the most important growth element in humanity: admitting you don't know everything, and learning, especially from other people, is the essence of personal growth. My teacher that week was Kelvin, but there wasn't a single lecture. It was his behavior. It was his attitude. I guess I heard about that a couple of times at home. But, it wasn't just *positive*.

It was as if he confirmed something I always believed, but started ignoring, even rebelled against, which I had attributed to *teenager disease*. It certainly was adolescence, but believe me, having a handicap truly complicates it further. What I always believed was I lived two lives: one that everyone watched and the other one I lived. Well, if they wanted to watch, maybe it was time to give them something to look at – on my terms.

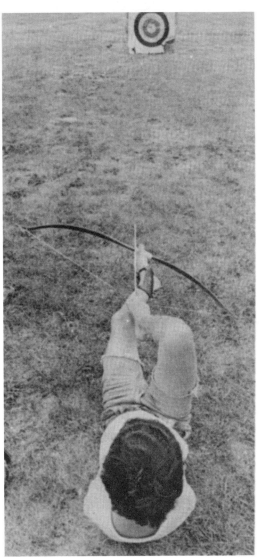

Archery at Camp Easter Seal

chapter twenty-two

the best of both worlds

After Camp Easter Seal, I attended Jazz Camp again and summed up my summer camping experience as a great success and symbolic of my new view. Because I believed I had a real talent for music, I wanted to be recognized for that talent alone. I couldn't control that, but I could control myself. What complicated things was my secret; I was going to be the Easter Seals *Timmy!* The problem was I couldn't tell a soul, as it wouldn't be announced until Christmas. I had a lot of time to think about it.

While I figured I had gone through a major change in my life, to most observers, I hadn't changed at all. Getting back to school, entering grade eleven, brought back familiar feelings, and I resumed some familiar habits. In fact, as my junior year plodded along, something quite bizarre happened.

My parents threatened to pull me out of band. It was a complete shock, but their motivation was no surprise at all. There are a ton of stories out there of people who credit sports, music, or some other non-academic pursuit for making them go to school. It was certainly true for me. Music did make me want to go to school, even though there was still *school*: classes, assignments, homework, and tests (boy, I don't miss school). Sometimes when people tell their inspirational stories, they sometimes leave it out because *school* isn't always fun. I especially hated math.

My math teacher and I didn't get along very well. As inspirational as my story may be, at the old YRHS, I was simply Alvin, one of a thousand kids who loved and hated their own subjects and teachers. The problem was, I was failing – for real. The bigger problem was that my blaming the teacher fell on completely deaf ears at home. If I didn't pass math, I was out of band. It didn't matter that we had a spring trip to Oklahoma to prepare for.

Look, all through this book, I have spouted my opinions, but I don't think I'm alone in my thinking. Everyone has a story of a teacher they hated or a subject they despised. (Sorry, your point is?) One of the most destructive attitudes in our new generation is, "That's not my fault!" (Again, your point?) I may have made reference to this before, but people who blame the world for their troubles need to get it together.

I realized I had no option. I swallowed my pride, and after my next math class, I waited behind and approached the teacher. I could tell he didn't like me.

I told him I needed help because I just wasn't catching on. He looked me right in the eyes and exclaimed, "It's because you're lazy. You may think it's because I hate you, or you might think it's because you hate math. Blame things all you want, but the truth is, your work shows you're lazy. This is grade eleven, young man; it isn't easy, and it's not supposed to be."

Wow, this sort of shocked me. He wasn't done.

"Alvin, I know your situation is complicated. I would never suggest any other teacher has done this, but taking it easy on you, giving you a break, all it will do is hurt you, not help you. Okay, school isn't always fun, but son, life isn't always fun. The difference is, in life, you don't have to take math forever. Here, if you don't pass math, you get no life!"

This guy was making scary sense. He still wasn't done.

"Look, have you ever considered this? I talked to Mr. McClary in the staff room last week and explained you were having some issues in my class. It wasn't official, just a conversation. But, I asked him if you were lazy. You should have seen him laugh. He told me he's never seen anyone work harder. It makes sense, though. You love band and music. Clearly, you don't love math. Too bad."

I hated lectures. I felt insulted he'd told Mr. McClary because this was private, I thought. He wasn't done.

"Take some advice, young man. Whatever you do to succeed in band, apply the same technique to math. Will it be fun? Not at first, but it will work. Isn't it true? You don't just play a song the first time and then quit, right? You play it over and over again until you get it right.

And don't you dare tell me that every song you've played in band, you loved, right? What did you do? You played it anyways because of your obligation to band and to Mr. McClary. Listen, I don't give two hoots what you think about me, but think about your obligation to school, all of it! Okay, this may not be easy. I don't really know you that well, but it seems to me, things not being easy doesn't strike me as something you have a problem with."

Done? Nope.

"I'll give you some extra work. I'll put it together just for you, but it's the only favor you get. Take it home and practice it just like you practice music. Who knows, you might surprise yourself and actually enjoy it."

No chance of the last part happening, but the first part, okay. I guess this made some sense. He was a smart teacher. So many students can't picture teachers being smart. It's probably because they remind them of another couple of idiots: parents.

Whatever happened, it worked. I pulled myself up from a serious failing grade to fifty-three percent. Okay, I pulled it up a lot. That'll give you an idea of how bad things were. More important, I learned a valuable lesson about schoolwork. No, it never was fun in math, but continuing in band *was* fun. My new study habits would not only help get me through grade eleven, they are habits I still use to this day.

There was also a residual effect. All that focus on school made the time go by, and just like that, Christmas came. The announcement was made, and I officially became the 1977 Easter Seals *Timmy*. The first time I dreamed of this was in 1967, when I met "Whipper" Billy Watson, a famous Canadian wrestler I had seen on television. I met him while on a day-trip from the Ontario Crippled Children's Center, a place I frequented over the years. We were taken to Lake Simco to go boating on some very big boats and afterwards there was a barbecue with a bunch of sports figures. The only one I cared about was *Whipper*. He had a great move where he'd use leg scissors around his opponents' necks to beat them into submission. I used that move to beat Dad when we wrestled, so he was an inspiration. I met him, but he sat at a VIP table with Ontario's 1967 *Timmy*. I was both jealous and impressed and secretly wished I could be *Timmy* one day.

It had come true, but I felt confused. What was I supposed to do? Most of the *Timmys'* responsibilities were simply promotional in nature: smiling for pictures, accepting donations, and thanking people for supporting Easter Seals. In some way, it seemed a bit shallow, but it was a good cause, and it was an honor. On the way to my first gig in Regina – a dinner and fundraiser at which I was required to thank those in attendance – Dad asked me what I was going to say when it was my turn at the podium. My somewhat dismissive answer was, "Thanks for your money."

I'm sure Mom and Dad were painfully accustomed to my typical teen attitude, but Dad ignored my tone and asked why I couldn't say more, an actual speech. I had no answer, but in a very enlightened moment, I didn't just dismiss Dad's question as I might typically have done. In fact, I even asked him what I would speak about. He had a short answer, "You."

Nobody in that car could have predicted what that simple word would lead to, especially me. Believe it or not, I was quite humble and needed more guidance from the folks.

Dad suggested I share the worst thing people did to me. In his mind that was feel sorry for me. He continued to say that when you feel sorry for someone, it demeans them, and ultimately, is an insult. He made sense. You know, whether we intend to or not, when we feel sorry for someone, we also see them as being less than we are. I have no desire to debate the equality of people because that argument is never won or lost; people will always believe what they believe based strongly on their own place in society. I believe people should receive respect, but I also believe our modern civilization is based on the "class system." If we follow that argument, people with disabilities are viewed as users, not givers, in our society. Clearly, I will argue that belief because I do it every day on stages all over the world. That mission, if you will, was born that day in the backseat of a 1972 Hornet Sportabout station wagon.

With Dad's, and Mom's, guidance, I wrote some thoughts on pages torn out of a *Hilroy* notebook. Thoughts about having no arms, about all the kids in Saskatchewan that faced similar challenges everyday, but most important, thoughts about victory, not defeat, of the human body and mind. I wrote about the huge difference between seeing no future and having hope. I encouraged those present not to feel sympathy for handicapped kids, but to feel privileged to be in a position to make a positive impact on their lives by their donations of time and money. I told them not to give out of guilt but out of a sense of celebration of the enduring power of the human spirit that can go so much further with encouragement, rather than the discouraging stigma that attaches itself to the label of "handicapped." I got a standing ovation.

After the dinner, I had lots of people thank me, but it was two people that stuck out more because of what they wanted. One man said he was from the Canadian Red Cross. He wanted to talk to my parents before he talked to me and had an idea for something very special that might interest me. The other was the executive director of the Saskatchewan Council for Crippled Children and Adults, who also ran Easter Seals in the province. He, too, wanted to talk to my parents but with me there.

By the time I made it to my folks, they were smiling in a way I had never seen before. It was pride, for sure. I got the hugs and kisses to prove it. But it was more. The man from Red Cross asked them if I could submit my name to attend an international camp in Norway that coming summer. I wasn't guaranteed to go but they didn't let just anyone apply either. Woohoo!

Shortly after that announcement, the director came over, introduced himself as Jim Wasylenkow. He shook my parents' hands and gave me a little hug. This man was pumped! He was very pleased with my speech, but he also had some good news. It seemed it was my lucky year. A group of very dedicated service club members calling themselves *Kinsmen* were organizing a huge fundraising event to benefit handicapped children in the province and Easter Seals would be one of the beneficiaries. He asked my parents if we could be in Saskatoon for the first weekend in March for the first ever *Telemiracle!* As of this writing *Telemiracle* has raised over sixty-one million dollars for one of the more worthy charities in the province, the Kinsmen Foundation. But in January of 1977, nobody had a clue what it was. There were plenty of cynics who doubted there would even be a show, let alone over twenty-nine of them as history has shown.

Telemiracle was Saskatchewan's first province-wide telethon. It took place from Saturday at 9:00 PM until Sunday at 5:00 pm on the CTV television network. A relatively well-known celebrity from a CTV show called *Funny Farm* (Canada's *Hee-Haw*), Blake Emmons, hosted the program. He was assisted by a host of big and small celebrities like Arte Johnson (*Laugh-In*), Lyle Wagner (*The Carol Burnett Show*), Jim Perry (game show host), and many other *names*. It also included many Saskatchewan celebrities and performers. The show ran *live* without any commercial breaks for twenty hours.

Because of my role as *Timmy,* I was on the show but was given no idea how much I would appear. My parents and I were invited to stay in Saskatoon for the weekend at the Holiday Inn (my first ever experience in a building taller than a grain elevator). We were VIP guests of the show. I made a token thirty-second appearance around 10:00 PM on the Saturday night, after which we could leave or stay backstage, whatever we liked. I insisted we stay at least until midnight because of the once in a lifetime opportunity. As humble and unassuming as my folks were, I think they enjoyed the experience too.

The next day, we were back on the set around noon. The amount of money being raised surprised everyone. I was told I'd be on sometime, but again, who was I, really? Besides, it was a blast just being there, rubbing shoulders with some very big-league stars.

Around 3:00 PM, Blake Emmons, who was quite a personality (you either loved or hated him) took me aside because he had an idea. He had been chatting with someone who knew of my musical talent, and he was very blunt with me. He told me the show had a chance of raising a million dollars, something *nobody* believed could happen (there were less than a million people in all of Saskatchewan), and that the last couple of hours, they really needed to push it. He believed I could have a significant impact on the emotions they were looking for. Here's my favorite part; he actually confided in me they had "milked" the sympathy stuff, and it was time to try something else, something that would impress upon people that donating wasn't because the recipients were these pathetic, helpless handicapped people, but friends, neighbors, and relatives – individuals who were a donation away from reaching the heights of their potential. *I* would be the proof of that potential.

At 4:00 PM, one hour from the finish, with an estimated five hundred thousand people or more watching, I was rolled out on a wheeled stage, sitting behind a full set of sparkling new drums. I was the guest drummer for a remarkable local band called "Prairie Fire." We played the blues standard, *Flip, Flop, and Fly*, and I was dead on. I was in heaven for four very short minutes. The experience was surreal. When the last beat was hit and the song was over, the live audience of over two thousand people in the Centennial Auditorium shot to their feet with an ovation that made the whole theatre shake, setting a vibration up my spine that I can still feel to this day.

Forty-five minutes later, calling out the numbers one at a time (a *Telemiracle* tradition) the seventh number said "one." It had happened. One million dollars!

I need you to know that I will never, *ever,* take credit for the total that day, but I believe Blake was dead-on, and I still feel that way. We give to charity for the doors of potential that are opened. We do it because all of us are a step away from needing the same kind of help we are asked to provide every day. No matter what the justification, or my strained humility, that day I became a part of the fabric of Saskatchewan history and *Telemiracle* folklore. I was famous overnight; not world famous or Canadian famous, but Saskatchewan famous, which for me, was my new world.

In Yorkton, it was even weirder. The local television, radio, and newspapers all wanted an interview. As I was learning, people were fascinated with my story. I used the opportunity, of course, to promote Easter Seals, and the organization was glowing in the recognition their little *Timmy* was providing.

And as if things couldn't get better, we received a letter from CBC, Canada's government-owned broadcasting network. They wanted to know if I'd like to be in a television documentary. Unbelievable.

A week later, another letter informed me I'd been chosen to travel to the camp in Norway for two weeks in July. I'd be part of a three-person delegation, one of whom had to be handicapped, to represent Canada – Canada, not just Yorkton or Saskatchewan – but the whole country at an international Red Cross camp. Twenty-seven countries would attend. It was an initiative of the King of Norway. His nephew was paralyzed in an accident, so he experienced first-hand the pathetic nature of accessibility, both physical and spiritual, for persons with disabilities. He built a camp and encouraged groups to use it for international gatherings of huge cultural significance.

That spring, our band traveled to Oklahoma for a huge music festival called "Tri-State." Not only did I win two gold medals for

the trombone and vocal solos I had performed in front of adjudicators, our school won one of three trophies (they called them Sweepstakes awards) for amassing the most points for participation and rankings in band, choir, and solo competitions. Trust me, this was a very big deal. That a Canadian band from a little town nobody ever heard of stole it right from under their noses was the icing on the cake.

Upon returning from Norway, my parents were amazed to discover I learned to toilet myself. For reasons that mystify me to this day, I had never mastered the art of the personal cleaning portion of a human bowel movement. Simple embarrassment became a major motivator in my learning while in transit to Norway. The tender and caring attitude of one of the other Red Cross delegates, Larry Galbraith, showed me that asking another guy for help isn't something to be concerned about. All I needed was for someone to undo then redo my pants button and zipper; the rest, well, I will leave that to another time.

As I referenced about *Telemiracle*, the same held true for Norway. I experienced true growth and maturity, and to nobody's surprise, I was different. I say nobody because the biggest revelation for me was realizing much of my feelings of isolation and intimidation were self-imposed.

If I could tell teenagers the most important lesson I learned, it would be when you feel like you have no friends, think again. Most important, realize that being popular doesn't mean you have to be *most popular*, and it doesn't mean you are the best person either.

That August, some band buddies were going camping (here we go with camping again), and they actually wanted me to come. My first instinct was to decline because I was sure they were just being polite and didn't want to offend me by exclusion. The other thought, of course, was they knew I couldn't come because my mom wasn't invited and camp meant Mom too. I will never forget how little credit I gave to my band buddies.

They knew I went to Norway, and therefore, probably assumed I had figured out the bathroom thing. So with my newly discovered confidence, I just flat-out asked them, "Do you guys know about the pants-thing?" They laughed and replied, "The whole school knows. You think we're that stupid?"

The whole school? That knowledge took me a minute to digest, but after I thought about it, my next thought was 'so what'? This was not a problem. I came back from whence I went in my mind and asked, "You don't mind helping me?"

"As long as we don't have to hold it!"

For the first time I could remember, I shared a laugh with some guys I thought disliked me, or at best, were indifferent. Then, I remembered how much time we spent together and what a pain in the ass I was. When I thought about that, no wonder nobody wanted to hang out with me. I wouldn't have hung out with me either.

I conned my parents into buying me a tent, and the following weekend, I went camping with my band buddies. Without going into too much detail, we did things I'd never done. I had more fun than I'd ever had with a bunch of guys. They were there all along but for reasons that teens thrive on without much logic, we had ignored the opportunity to get to really know each other.

The year 1977 was turning out to be quite a year. What made it that much better was another typical scenario you may identify with; I was about to start my senior year of high school. No matter where one finds their life occurring, reaching the final year of high school is universal. For some, it may end in the hollow feeling of dropping out. For others, it may be just one more year to endure until the agony is over. For yet a different group, it is a year filled with the stress of maintaining high enough marks to allow acceptance into a prestigious college or university. For me, it was about making up for lost time and reaching for the potential I'd been hearing about at home for years. One last chance…I could see the finish line!

chapter twenty-three

proof

There is no question that my experiences of the past year changed me, and if the bulk of change was maturity, that was cool. Whatever it was, it wasn't just one thing. I do believe my trip to Norway definitely redefined who I was. The timing couldn't have been better.

As you've already read in this book, these stories are more than just autobiographical; at least, I hope so. I've also made many observations – even if I must admit the era from which I arose dates my feelings substantially.

It seems so funny that today, so many more young people have traveled, a lot of them, extensively. That is a good thing, but selfishly, it makes my generation's stories of travel seem so lame. Going to Norway in 1977 was actually a really big deal. Today, teenagers take school trips during spring break to many European countries, Asia, or further, like it's no big deal. I'm not suggesting they don't appreciate it, but as they say, "The times, they are a changing."

One thing that never changes, or I hope it won't, is how vital it is for people of all ages to understand their relevance. I believe 1977 wasn't specifically about Norway, my being *Timmy,* or becoming an overnight celebrity because of *Telemiracle.* I think it was about everything I did before 1977 finally bared its fruit. As you've seen, the "N" is for *Never Give Up.* As inspiring as that may be, let's really consider what it means.

Never give up literally means *never*! I don't want to make any assumptions here, but so often, people see what I can do with amazement but may not consider how hard all of this really was. I'm definitely not bragging now. I am constantly amazed at how people want success...now.

We've all played the "if I won the lottery" game, and without exception, people claim it wouldn't change them. Impossible. More common sense again, but isn't the payoff better when one earns it?

My dedication was paying off. All of the pain and sacrifice seemed almost nonexistent as I saw my life changing. In fact, it was finally occurring to me that all the challenges were in themselves, necessary. Friedrich Nietzsche, a German philosopher and writer once said, "That which does not kill me makes me stronger." Exactly. He was a deep thinker, that fellow. He was also proof that the clues others have toward life's mysteries are worth paying attention to. Ironically, unless we have proof, faith is a tough nut.

My faith was becoming stronger everyday and not in a religious way. Let's face it, even Mother Teresa needed a bit of a payoff. With all her sacrifice, she received so much back. For her (I'm assuming), the payoff wasn't a new BMW or condo in the Caribbean. It was knowing her dedication made a difference. You have to admit, everyone, even someone like Mother Teresa, needs to feel relevance.

As I entered my senior year of high school, it seemed to me that, where most seniors feel excitement at the prospect of graduation, I was, for the first time, beginning to see past the end of school. I had never done this before. I probably wasn't even conscious of it, but in looking back, I can now identify it.

There was another corny expression: "Live every day like it's your last." I agree with the sentiment, but how do you do that? My guess comes from what I was feeling that fall of 1977. I would never walk this path again. The road would take me to places I could actually get to, not just dream of. Norway taught me that. Of course, part of the focus would be academics, but something inside of me said my future was in music. It wasn't the romantic in me as much as the practical conclusion of my limited career choices. I often joked that when using your feet like I do, you don't plan a career in dentistry. "Open wider!" I don't think so.

I want to make a short reference back to our trip to Oklahoma in the spring of 1977. This music festival was a very big deal. In our world, it was the emotional equivalent of that which was portrayed in the classic movie, *Hoosiers*, a movie documentary focusing on two boys trying to make and sustain a spot on highly competitive high school basketball teams.

Our little crew from rural Canada rode a bus for four days, with stops enroute for concerts at high schools, where band director buddies of Mr. McClary taught (remember, he was American). We had extra practices for months, sold caseloads of chocolate bars to raise money, and each member also worked on their solos because if you recall, the big trophy was for overall points. What each soloist did in their individual competition counted towards the band and choir as a whole. We were very stressed because of such high expectations from ourselves, our school, our families, and indeed, all of Yorkton. But as we traveled together, something was building that we probably failed to notice at first. It was pride.

We all played our best in the solo competitions. As I mentioned, I won my sections in voice and trombone. In fact, I beat one hundred ninety-six trombonists in my class and even received an adjudicators' award for performance of the day in both categories. I wasn't the only one. Our band members were inspired. So many of us won that we were collectively feeling the impossible now seemed within reach.

As groups, we were very focused. The performances by our concert choir, concert band, and one of two jazz bands took top honors in our category (based on school size). In the biggest surprise of all, our little marching band, comprised of fifty-five of our usual one hundred (not everyone could make the trip), won our category, besting many other greater-sized bands, including one band with two hundred kids. On the final night of the festival, there was a collective gathering of all the participants to hear a couple of guest college bands. With great ceremony and drama, the Yorkton Regional High School was proclaimed a Sweepstakes award winner. The pure joy was something I had never experienced before.

What it taught me was the most important thing. That night, we won. Many nights, we lost. True, we put in a great deal of effort both preparing for the festival and playing our hearts out while we were there. So had the other bands, I suppose. Perhaps the ultimate difference was pride. Did they have pride? Of course, they did, but something, whatever it was, made the ultimate difference.

Maybe it *was* recognizing this was a true *once-in-a-lifetime* experience. What that brings to the human dynamic is profound. It becomes all the more powerful when applied as a group or team. Okay, this isn't original thinking, but for me, at seventeen years old, it spoke to me.

I liked the concept so much, I was able to practice this new feeling everyday to the point where it became part of my subconscious. Ironically, I'm not as good at it today as I was then. If I were to guess why, it might be because life was less complicated then. In another way, it probably had to do with simply being young. There's one other possibility as well.

When it came to band, I had something to prove. I believe many thought I got into band, even won solo competitions, because of sympathy. It's just a feeling I had. Whether it was right or wrong, it's what drove me everyday. That feeling transferred from band to school. I went from a sixty percent average in grade eleven to seventy-nine percent in my senior year. My biggest improvement was in dreaded math, which proved that teacher's concept about practicing being the same as studying.

People often say it's easy to work at something you love. I think working at something you don't love is worth the challenge. In fact, that's exactly what you do. Proving something isn't solely about ego. I think it has a powerful connection to understanding what our lives are all about. Rather than working to find an answer, how about working to ask more questions, and in the process, give our lives their own renaissance.

I really hadn't thought about this until grade twelve because I was too busy focusing on what was wrong with me. When I took a step back and had a look; I had a lot to be proud of.

I could play trombone, the drums, Frisbee, marbles, hide and seek, ping pong, putt-putt golf, soccer, football, floor hockey, road hockey, and table-top hockey. I could read, write, type, and draw. I could cook, vacuum, mow the lawn, and shovel snow. I could brush my teeth and hair, shave, shower, and go to the bathroom alone. I could

fish, skip stones, put up a tent, and shoot bows and arrows and a gun. I
could skip, run, jump rope (not hold it though), and skate. I could sing,
tap dance, drive a boat, drive a car, and drive my parents crazy. I could
talk and listen. I could smile and cry. I had kissed a few girls and even
held their hands. I could open a combination lock standing on one foot,
use a screwdriver and a hammer. I mean, the more I thought about it,
look how much I learned to do, and I was only seventeen years old?

Try it! Sit down and make a list of *everything* you can do, even
if it seems some of those things are trivial. I think you'll be surprised
at not only how long the list is but how thinking about it makes you
feel. A major challenge I hope you take on after reading this book is
to try and take fewer things for granted. By the way, to get back on
track here, don't you also have a few memories of when you proved
your abilities to others?

Maybe that's the key. When some of the smartest people in the
country tell you and/or your parents you'll never be able to do anything,
you have a simple choice, really. Believe them or prove them wrong.
This was cool stuff. The more I proved to myself, the more I proved to
the world, the more I wanted to try, and the more confidence I gained
in the process.

My senior year of high school was something I not only learned
to appreciate every day, but so many years later. I am still thankful for
every day. You couldn't have written a better script if you tried. I was
getting invited to social events and parties and even started *going out
for coffee* (I drank hot chocolate…couldn't stand coffee), a high school
tradition, right? My parents, seeing my progression, were giving me
more space and trust. They even bought me my first car, a 1972 Pinto. It
was gold with matching *fun-fur* accents inside. As rotten the reputation
the Pinto would gain and as ugly as it was, I loved it.

I spent almost a week with a film crew from CBC television
who produced a documentary called, *Alvin…His Best Foot Forward.*
They even spent a fair chunk of time at the school. Being followed
around by a film crew definitely had an impact on my peers and me.
The documentary was shown on the network across Saskatchewan on
Boxing Day, 1977. It was so well received, it made its prime-time debut
across Canada on CBC, Easter Monday, 1978.

My music continued to amaze both my family and me. In March, our jazz band made an appearance on *Telemiracle* (I had some pull). Later that month, we won the provincial high school stage band competition, which qualified us for the Canadian Stage Band Finals in Winnipeg, Manitoba. We took third in the country and surpassed our expectations. In the definition of surpassed expectations, I was named lead chair in Canada's All Star High School Stage Band. It's true. I was recognized, along with twenty-four peers, as having reached the pinnacle of achievement for high school jazz musicians. I reached the summit of my Everest at seventeen.

In May, our bands and choirs reached theirs, winning every category at the prestigious Kinsmen Band Festival in Moose Jaw, Saskatchewan. If you've never heard of it, this real town, forty minutes west of Regina, hosted a festival that had no rivals across Canada. To win there, was indeed, a very big deal. The trophy cabinet outside our band and choir rooms would need an expansion after the year we were having.

In June, I was bestowed with one of only five honor awards for the entire school (not the *honor* roll, that's different). It was for involvement in extracurricular activities. On the night of our official graduation, *The Class of 1978,* I received the Margaret Frieheit Award of Excellence. Named after a very special student who passed away years earlier, its recipient was chosen by the graduating students themselves. My classmates picked *me!*

The emotion I felt that night was about as complicated as it got. As I climbed on stage, and Mr. Matthews placed the medal around my neck, I was both humbled and embarrassed. I thought everybody hated me. I was wrong. It's good to be wrong. It's even better to be able to admit it.

I received a letter informing me I was accepted as a first year Broadcasting student at Mount Royal College in Calgary the same week as my graduation. If there was ever a reason to celebrate, this was certainly the one, but I also realized something else. This whole year had been a celebration, and it wasn't simply because I (and we) had collected some hardware.

I can't stress enough another particularly obvious observation. It is theoretically impossible to succeed, let alone be the best, without dedication, perseverance, but most of all, *practice*. It kills me how simple that seems. I also alluded to this earlier, but that means with everything, not just in my case, the trombone. It is the habit it creates. When that habit extends to other sectors of your life, you have achievement. With a bit of good karma, you may even have victory.

There are many who believe that graduating from high school signifies an ending. For me, graduation was the ultimate proof I had been looking for all my life. True, the proof was aimed at all those who gave me grief, but ultimately, the most important proof was for me. To have proof means everything. It not only gives you a tremendous feeling of satisfaction, it becomes an appetite or thirst for more. Now, I asked myself, how far could I go?

chapter twenty-four
time for me to fly

In August of 1978, I packed up my 1974 green American Motors Hornet Sportabout station wagon to begin a new chapter of my life. When I recall it, to this day, it still gives me a shiver. I should probably explain. In July, I wrecked my Pinto when, during a short lapse of proper judgment – trying to beat a friend of mine (who owned a very fast and new Camaro) to a party we were headed to. I determined the destined location required a shortcut. A tree jumped in front of me, and I used the little Ford as a weapon of self-defense. At least I didn't hit it while traveling backwards, ha! (Pinto joke)

Mom, Dad, the Hornet and Me

Seriously, I learned a very valuable lesson that night, one that was accompanied with yet another range of emotions, none of them pleasant. Simple recognition of my pending move and good insurance saw my very agitated father struggle with his own emotions. With remarkable compromise, he found me the Hornet. Ironically, if I had the Hornet that night, I probably wouldn't have hit the tree. The Pinto had rack and pinion steering, not power assisted, and I hit the tree while taking a turn too fast. The heat of July and no air-conditioning made the plastic steering wheel slippery. My foot just slipped off the wheel. Bang! As simple as that.

The Hornet had power steering. We added a leather wrap for the steering wheel. The bonus was, it was a wagon. I could fit a ton of stuff in that car, even my whole drum set.

Of all the things I do with my feet, driving seems to surprise people the most, especially people behind the counter at the car rental agencies. I can't lie. I do enjoy their reaction, although one time in England, they refused me a car. I'll leave my reaction to your imagination. Needless to say, the executives at the car rental company heard about it, and in a very classy move, made sure it didn't happen again.

As you've probably figured out, but I will repeat it again, using my feet was instinctive, but the stuff I wanted to do was very rarely designed for use of feet. Using a can opener (pretty innocent), driving a car (different scenario). The thing was, I wanted to drive, and nothing would stop me. That was the theory anyway.

Don't get me wrong. I firmly believe that driving is an *earned privilege,* not a right. Frankly, a ton of people *with* hands shouldn't have their license at all. I was completely prepared to follow the rules, but what happens when they haven't thought of a rule because, well, they just never thought a guy without arms would want to drive? *They,* by the way, would be my biggest problem, not driving.

We had a small boat at Crystal Lake. I learned to drive it without any difficulty at all. Steer with my left foot and use the hand throttle and gearshift with my right for practice. My father used to let me sit on the passenger seat of our car (never when Mom was there) and steer, while he used the gas. I believe that was pivotal because I learned the *feel* of a car. To this day, I can jump into a rental, even models I've never driven, and recognize the *way* a car handles. With respect, if everyone took driving as serious as I do, we'd have way less problems. But I'm not bragging. People take driving for granted. In 1976, I couldn't.

This was *before* specialized controls, and they really weren't the issue. I wanted to (here we go one more time) *prove* myself. I signed up for in-class driver training, and being an enrolled student at YRHS, I couldn't be turned away. Using my newly found studying techniques, I worked harder than ever. I literally aced the exams, scoring one hundred percent. There were some tentative discussions about possibly altering a vehicle, but once I passed the course, I was automatically sent a learner's permit from the motor licensing division of the government. Nowhere on my application did I mention I had no arms. I wasn't trying to hide it; I didn't think it mattered.

As I had learned, practice was the key to everything. My motivation was clear. I bugged my parents constantly to take me driving, and they usually complied. Honestly, it was kind of brutal having Dad as my instructor. He was a great driver, although his extremely high expectations could wear on you, but it was good thing. I needed to be *perfect*. Dad made an additional rule: no driver's test until I passed Dad's test. Yikes!

Not to bait you, but I plan on diving deeper into this subject in my next book. Really, it doesn't matter if you don't know all the details, but after passing Dad's test, I booked a time for the official one. When I showed up, I was refused the test because someone in head office caught wind of this and wanted to either make certain everything was properly handled or justify their mundane, bureaucratic position in the public service (no comment on which side I lean towards). No matter the reason and again, to sidestep the longer (and quite fascinating) version, they sent some manager with clout to test me. In a moment in his life that he has probably recounted a few times, I passed – one hundred percent – again.

I started driving as much as I could, without my own car. Even I didn't really consider what I was doing was any big deal. My schedule, along with my improved attitude and acceptance of added responsibility, all contributed to my parents buying the Pinto. I had my heart set on a new Trans-Am, just like the one Burt Reynolds drove in *Smokey and the Bandit*. In a weird twist of life, my wife Darlene's ex-husband had the same car, but it was gold, not black as in the movie. They had a new one at the Pontiac dealership in Yorkton that I coveted; it, too, was gold. Weird.

So, I got the Pinto, not my choice, and wrecked it, also not my choice. I ended up with the Hornet, still not my choice, but I had long since learned not to look a gift horse in the mouth (isn't that an odd cliché?). As I already mentioned, lots of stuff fit in the new car (not new but new to me). Even though I didn't own much, what I did, I excitedly packed and prepared for the trip to Calgary.

I know millions of young people do this every year. You may have or will someday, but leaving home for the pursuance of one's own life is, as far as I'm concerned, why we have children. I know there are a couple of other reasons, but really, the ultimate objective is to give them the gift of freedom and curiosity to *find themselves*. I believe Mom and Dad gave me more gifts than many people get. I don't mean the ones in pretty packages with a bow.

Not only did they take me in when nobody wanted me, they raised me as a Law, a third child, and as much a member of the family as my brothers. Their way was not new. It had to be adapted somewhat, but the objective for me was always centered on that inevitable day. When I think back, I had no real clue of the significance of the gift of letting go. It must have been a tough day for them...or not. (When my son Vance moved out, it was a good day, trust me!)

They handled it well. The moment that took over eighteen years to arrive came and went in a flash, or more specifically, a honk and a wave. Did you have a honk and wave? If not, and I'm certainly not suggesting your life must be meaningless without one, but the honk and wave is truly profound, isn't it?

Pulling away from that curb, turning right onto Yorkton's Fifth Avenue, driving two blocks down to Darlington, then a dozen or so more streets and a left onto Gladstone, passing the Yorkton Regional High School (which I smiled at like the Cheshire cat), then a few more blocks to Broadway and a right turn to the edge of town began the journey of discovery. It's just weird how that feels. When you pull away and go, you're not coming back "in a couple of hours." The night before, you slept in your bed. I had the exact same bedroom and furniture since 1963. That next night, I would sleep in a new bedroom and home for the first time in my life. More important, I was going alone! I know that's big for everyone, but please, as *okay* and *normal* as I profess to be, I had no arms. This was a big deal.

I had never driven that far alone (there were countless family car trips...without the built-in DVD entertainment center, I might add).

I had *never* been to Calgary. I saw pictures. (They rode horses there, right?)

I will never forget my first glimpse of the skyline. It had tall buildings that didn't say "POOL" on the side. There was this really cool tower with a big *pod* on the top. I heard it had a restaurant that spun. That couldn't be good for digestion, could it? However, the best part, the absolute most stunning sight, was the mountains. They were beautiful. The city was beautiful. Life was beautiful!

Giddy is one word that comes to mind but I felt more than that. It was joy! I remembered as the city grew bigger, the joy morphed into – not fear – but close. It was the reality of being in a very big city – alone. Although I had a map and directions, it was still intimidating. I knew what helped me relax when I was intimidated: music. I was listening to my tape deck, a habit I formed living in a town with limited radio and being on a trip that took almost eleven hours. I had long since listened to all my tapes, a few times, so I turned on the radio. It was then I discovered something ultra-cool. I saw a billboard for *CJAY-92!* The sign said, "Calgary's Original Rock Station." And then the best part: "In Clean, Crisp FM." FM! All right! I heard FM before, but had never pushed that button on my stereo. When I did, the whole world changed. My stereo sounded great. The first song I heard in Calgary on FM radio was *Saturday Night's Alright* [sic] *For Fighting* by Elton John. Guess what day it was? Saturday!

At that precise moment, I was stopped by a lengthy red light. As I sat there, with the skyline in front of me in the distance, that great song playing on the radio, plus not needing to steer, I gleefully started tapping my foot on the top of the steering wheel.

(Dramatic pause)

I was pretty distracted, but not enough that I lost track of my surroundings.

There was a small car stopped at the light beside me. When I glanced at it, something wasn't right. It wasn't overly obvious, but it wasn't right. The car was leaning. Maybe someone "large" was on the passenger side. None of my business. Still, I was curious by nature, so I glanced again, still tapping my foot, rocking away. It *was* leaning, but it wasn't someone large. There were three guys, relatively big,

I guess, but that's not what caused the car to lean. Their faces were smooshed against the passenger windows, just like little kids do to make a mark. They were just staring away in a complete trance. What were they looking at? They couldn't possibly know I had no arms. I was in my car.

But I was tapping my foot on the wheel. When I actually got it, the light coincidentally turned green, so as to not betray my mood, I waved and drove away!

Dad *was* right! I would get stared at for the rest of my life. I could either stay home or figure out a way to deal with it. Well, I didn't stay home. I finally figured out a way to deal with it. For the very first time, and I know because of how clear this became as I drove off, I understood *The Choice!*

We can't pick how we're born. We can't always pick the things that happen to us, although the choices we make sometimes cause those things to happen. We *can* pick our *attitude!*

You know, that's how this book started. *A for Alvin; A for Attitude.*

Alvin's Laws Of Life are not foolproof. In fact, it *is* the foolish who believe they can just read this book and that's enough. You have to act on the ideas and practice them – everyday. You also have an assignment.

Sit down and write your own Laws. You can use your name if you like, but if you have a really long or complicated name, blame your mom, not me. Here's the key. You have to be spontaneous. I wrote the first *Laws* in fifteen minutes. I have refined them over time. That's allowed, but eventually, they have to be left alone. Then you have to put them up, like in the bathroom. I did that when I was twenty years old. Not the *Laws*. I received a handmade plaque from an older lady who saw me on *Telemiracle* and really admired my attitude. She gave me something she thought fit who I was.

It said:

I am not afraid of tomorrow,

For I have seen yesterday,

And I love today.

I hung it my bathroom so it would be the first thing I would
see every morning.

Twenty-five years later, I have my *Law's* in my office now. Not because I'm conceited, but because everyone, and I mean *everyone*, needs to take some time, put your feet up, and bring the joy back in our lives and by taking these 5 steps you too can successfully overcome anything.

Cheers,

Alvin

I need a book of its own to acknowledge all the people who have been a part of this, my first book. For the sake of brevity, not my specialty, I want to highlight a few of the truly special.

This may be my story, but it was really inspired by Jack and Hilda Law. If they were alive, they'd probably be uncomfortable with me having a book, period. They never sought recognition or any spotlight, but they deserved it. I have struggled, largely unsuccessfully, at reaching their level of humility, but without their love, sacrifice, and unwavering faith, there simply wouldn't be the Alvin this book is about because there wouldn't be the unbelievable life I have lived.

There's a line that says a lot of men search for a partner just like their mother. Well, there was definitely only one Hilda Law, but when I met Darlene, I got the shivers. She is my wife, business partner, critic, pal, and lover. In fact, she is so many things, she is hard to define. She may have entered my life during my thirties, but she has forever been part of my soul and will be for eternity. She performed CPR on my fledgling speaking business; without asking, became full-time stepmom to Vance when he was ten; sacrificed every holiday with her family to be with mine for too long; she, in essence, set aside her identity for ours. This may be overstated, but everything she has been and continues to be could never be stated enough.

For Vance, you need to know, my son, that your sacrifices are not lost in the shuffle. Being a professional speaker is very much like being an entertainer and "the road" is part of the tradeoff…not an easy one. I had to choose my clients over you too many times, and although my absence wasn't the end of your life, you must have questioned the point of that life so many times. As I have found the purpose of my life, so too, will you. Thanks for all you gave up by allowing me to pursue my dreams. I owe ya!

I thought I would always be a broadcaster, but one fateful day in 1981, I quit my radio gig to visit schools as a speaker. Thanks to Lee Bussard for making that call. Lee is gone now, and I miss what he gave me. His gift for me was not just speaking but who he was. I miss *Swanney River* and all the laughs, my friend.

To Debbie Elicksen and her team for making my words the dream of a published book.

The photos on the cover were taken by pal and master photographer, Mitch. Thanks for your creativity, and to you and Geraldine, thanks for capturing the special moments in our life that adorn the walls of our home. You are both truly gifted.

Finally, to everyone who has hung in there as this decade-long project has finally been completed. You know who you are.

A toast of the good stuff,

Alvin

Vance, Alvin, and Darlene

about the author

Alvin Law

Over 13,000 babies were deformed in the early 1960s because of a morning sickness drug: *thalidomide.* Alvin Law was born without arms after his birth mother, thinking it was completely safe, used just a couple of the tiny pills. Their lives were forever altered.

Yet, what may have become a tragic life story did not turn out that way. Today, Alvin is not only a completely independent, remarkably successful professional speaker, but proof that out of nothing can arise one of the most inspiring stories you will ever witness.

Faced with no hope in their minds, Alvin's birth family courageously gave him up for adoption, hoping and praying that someone else may be more prepared for the welfare of this pitiful newborn. Their prayers were answered.

Hilda Law was a fifty-five year old foster mother, who, along with her husband, Jack, took in neglected and abused children, loved and encouraged them back from their hopelessness, and through social service programs, sent them to couples yearning for adoptions. They were truly special people.

One day in 1960, the most disturbing case they had ever seen was presented to them. Take in a sickly, deformed baby whose future seemed certain. He would never possess any quality of life, but he deserved more. Who knew?

Not only did Hilda nurse him back to health, her intuition said, lurking inside this impossible scenario was hope. Through the Law's faith, dedication, and infinite belief, little Alvin learned to use his feet for hands. This book is the account of that story.

Alvin attended regular schools in a day when handicapped children were relegated to institutions, or at best, schools that segregated them from the normal students. Remarkable teachers saw his potential and worked with the family to search any possibility to expand on it.

Then like a genie in a bottle, Alvin was recognized for his musical ability, and he joined the band. Within an impossibly short time, he became an award-winning musician and graduated from high school with honors. He then graduated, again with honors, from college and embarked on a career in Broadcasting.

In 1981, he took a hiatus from disc jockeying in FM radio and joined a company that, through a federal grant of the International Year of Disabled Persons, conducted awareness seminars in hundreds of schools across the province of Alberta, Canada. Thus began his adventures in the field of motivational speaking.

After working for the Saskatchewan Abilities Council, an Easter Seals agency, he ran, unsuccessfully, for a seat in the provincial legislature. He also worked in advertising, public relations, and the civil service of his beloved home province.

In 1985, his pride and joy, Vance, was born. He quit a lucrative government job in 1988 to fulfill a long-time dream and created AJL Communications Ltd. His career as a full-time professional speaker was born.

Since 1976, Alvin has played a direct role in raising over $150,000,000 for charity. He's also dabbled in acting, playing a role in a quirky creative film *Julien: Donkey Boy* and in a life highlight, played an armless preacher in an episode of the hit television series *The X-Files*.

Alvin often says he always knew angels existed. In 1991, he met one, and in 1993, he married Darlene. In 1995, his son Vance came to live with them. In 2000, they moved to Calgary, Alberta, where they now reside with Jazper, Ray, and Dexter the dogs, and Trixie the cat.

order form

book: alvin's laws of life

Company _____

Address _____

City/Province/State _____ Postal/Zip _____

Telephone _____ Fax _____

Contact Name _____

Email _____

☐ Prepaid (cheque enclosed) ☐ Invoice Required

☐ Credit Card

Type _____ Number _____

Signature _____

Number of Books @ $20 CDN/$15 US each: _____

Shipping and Handling ($5 CDN/$6US per book _____

Order total $ _____

GST $ _____

Total $ _____

Special Instructions: _____

_____

_____

Check or money order to:

AJL Communications Ltd.
273 Sunmills Drive S.E.
Calgary, Alberta, Canada T2X 3E6
www.alvinlaw.com

what is your alvin story?

Anyone who has ever met Alvin Law or seen him speak will never forget the experience. He has made a positive impression on many.

Do you have an Alvin story you wish to share? If you do, we'd love to hear it.

Send your story to:

AJL Communications Ltd.
273 Sunmills Drive S.E.
Calgary, Alberta
T2X 3E6
adlaw@telusplanet.net